# DISCRIMINATION IN THE WORKPLACE

# DISCRIMINATION IN THE WORKPLACE
## *A Practical Guide*

Julian Hemming, MA, LLM, Solicitor
Kate Mason, LLB, Solicitor
David Fisher, MA, Solicitor

*Employment Law Group*
*Nicholson Graham & Jones*

JOHN WILEY & SONS
Chichester • New York • Weinheim • Brisbane • Singapore • Toronto

Published in 1997 by John Wiley & Sons Ltd,
Baffins Lane, Chichester,
West Sussex PO19 1UD, England

National        01243 779777
International    (+44) 1243 779777
e-mail (for orders and customer service enquiries): cs-books@wiley.co.uk
Visit our Home Page on http://www.wiley.co.uk
or http://www.wiley.com

*Other Wiley Editorial Offices*

John Wiley & Sons, Inc., 605 Third Avenue
New York, NY 10158-0012, USA

VCH Verlagsgesellschaft mbH, Pappelallee 3,
D-69469 Weinheim, Germany

Jacaranda Wiley Ltd, 33 Park Road, Milton,
Queensland 4064, Australia

John Wiley & Sons (Asia) Pte Ltd, 2 Clementi Loop #02-01,
Jin Xing Distripark, Singapore 0512

John Wiley & Sons (Canada) Ltd, 22 Worcester Road,
Rexdale, Ontario M9W IL1, Canada

**British Library Cataloguing in Publication Data**

A catalogue record for this book is available from the British Library

ISBN 0-471-96580-4

Typeset in Times by Poole Typesetting (Wessex) Ltd, Bournemouth, Dorset
Printed and bound in Great Britain by Biddles Ltd, Guildford and King's Lynn
This book is printed on acid-free paper responsibly manufactured from sustainable forestation, for which at least two trees are planted for each one used for paper production.

# CONTENTS

# Appendices

# Index                                                325

# PREFACE

We would like to acknowledge the advice and encouragement given in the preparation of this work from our colleagues in the Employment Law Group including, Anthony Walker (Senior Partner), Kevin McCavish and Sola Coard. We would also like to thank Nicholson Graham & Jones's Director of Administration, Michael Bennett and Jenny Hassell Smith and Fiona Muxlow for commenting on the text.

Many others have helped in the preparation of this work and we are particularly grateful to Lynn Ravenhill, Jackie Bagnaro, Angela Key and the indefatigable word processing team at Nicholson Graham & Jones who between them have had to deal with the many drafts produced by the three of us.

Thanks also go to Sue Joshua of John Wiley & Sons.

*Julian Hemming, MA, LLM, Solicitor*
*Kate Mason, LLB, Solicitor*
*David Fisher, MA, Solicitor*

*Employment Law Group*
*Nicholson Graham & Jones*
*110 Cannon Street*
*London EC4N 6AR*

2 December 1996

# INTRODUCTION

While this book aims to provide a guide primarily for employers and managers to the law and good practice relating to race, sex and disability discrimination, it is also intended to be a useful source of information for practitioners who advise on discrimination. This book deals mainly with discrimination in the workplace; it does not cover in any detail discrimination in education, housing and in the provision of goods, facilities and services which are also covered by the anti-discrimination legislation. In Appendix 4 we list useful contacts from whom further information on these subjects can be obtained.

## The discrimination industry

Figures published in the 1995 Report of the Advisory Conciliation and Arbitration Service (ACAS) show that 1995 was a record year for industrial tribunal cases. The total number of cases was in the region of 91,500, up 15 per cent on 1994, itself a record year. The ACAS figures show an increase of 9 per cent in sex discrimination cases. This increase in discrimination cases may be a consequence of the removal of the ceiling on compensation in cases of race, sex and, now, disability discrimination. In recent well publicised sex discrimination cases awards have been made in excess of £140,000.

The introduction of the Disability Discrimination Act 1995 (which came into force on 2 December 1996) and the growing campaign for legislation to outlaw age discrimination indicate that discrimination in the workplace is a matter which employers can no longer afford to ignore. In addition to hurting employers' pockets, such claims can cause unrest and dissatisfaction among the workforce as well as being a source of unwanted and embarrassing publicity.

We hope that this book will help to reduce the number of claims.

This book reflects the law as at 2 December 1996.

# ABBREVIATIONS

### Race discrimination

| | |
|---|---|
| RRA | Race Relations Act 1976 |
| CRE | Commission for Racial Equality |
| CRE Code | The CRE Code of Practice issued on 1 April 1994 under s 47 RRA |

### Sex discrimination

| | |
|---|---|
| EqPA | The Equal Pay Act 1970 (as amended) |
| SDA | Sex Discrimination Act 1975 |
| EOC | The Equal Opportunities Commission |
| The ET Directive | The Equal Treatment Directive 76/207/EEC |
| EC Code of Practice | European Commission Recommendation and Code of Practice on Measures to Combat Sexual Harassment |

### Disability discrimination

| | |
|---|---|
| Code of Practice | Code of Practice for the Elimination of Discrimination in the Field of Employment against Disabled Persons (published by HMSO) |
| DDA | Disability Discrimination Act 1995 |
| Employment Disability Regulations | Disability Discrimination (Employment) Regulations 1996 |
| Meaning of Disability Regulations | Disability Discrimination (Meaning of Disability) Regulations 1996 |
| NDC | National Disability Council |
| NIDC | Northern Ireland Disability Council |

### Maternity rights

| | |
|---|---|
| EWC | expected week of childbirth |
| NDR | notified date of return |

### Courts

| | |
|---|---|
| ECJ | European Court of Justice |
| EAT | Employment Appeal Tribunal |

## Case references

| | |
|---|---|
| IRLR | Industrial Relations Law Reports |
| ICR | Industrial Case Reports |
| AC | Law Reports, Appeal Cases |
| All ER | All England Law Reports |
| COIT | Industrial Tribunal folio number |
| SCOIT | Scottish Industrial Tribunal folio number |
| CMLR | Common Market Law Reports |

## General statutes and statutory instruments

| | |
|---|---|
| ERA | Employment Rights Act 1996 |
| TUPE | Transfer of Undertakings (Protection of Employment) Regulations 1981 (as amended) |
| TURERA | Trade Union Reform and Employment Rights Act 1993 |

# TABLES

## Table of UK Cases

## Table of European Cases

## Table of Statutes

## Table of Statutory Instruments

## Table of EC Directives

## Table of EC Treaties and Conventions

# PART I
*Discrimination – The Law*

# CONTENTS OF CHAPTER 1

## *Race Discrimination*

# 1.   RACE DISCRIMINATION

## Relevant law

### Acts of Parliament

#### Race Relations Act 1976

The RRA applies to the whole of Great Britain (but not to Northern Ireland) and is the most commonly applied statute in respect of claims for race discrimination. The RRA enables individuals to bring claims for unlawful race discrimination in an industrial tribunal against their employer, co-workers and others.

#### Local Government Act 1988

This Act places a general duty on local authorities to eliminate unlawful race discrimination.

#### The Race Relations (Remedies) Act 1994

This Act has provided industrial tribunals with the power, as from 3 July 1994, to award unlimited compensation to victims of race discrimination.

### Statutory instruments

#### The Race Relations (Offshore Employment) Order 1987 (SI 1987/929)

This statutory instrument brings within the scope of the RRA certain employment concerned with off-shore workers involved in the exploration of natural resources.

#### Race Relations (Interest on Awards) Regulations 1994 (SI 1994/1748)

This statutory instrument provides that as from 1 August 1994 industrial tribunals are empowered to award interest which accrues on a daily basis on compensation awarded for race discrimination.

## Code of practice

*The Commission for Racial Equality Statutory Code of Practice*

The Commission for Racial Equality (CRE) is a statutory body established under the RRA to promote racial equality and to enforce the RRA. It has been in existence for 20 years. In 1984, the CRE issued a statutory code of practice for the elimination of racial discrimination and for the promotion of equality of opportunity in employment. The CRE code gives practical guidance on the provisions of the RRA. Whilst the CRE code does not impose legal obligations, its provisions are far reaching because an industrial tribunal must take any relevant paragraph of the CRE code into account in deciding any question of race discrimination.

## The forms of race discrimination

Race discrimination may occur in three forms: direct, indirect and victimisation.

## Direct race discrimination

Direct race discrimination is governed by s 1(1)(a) RRA. This occurs where because of his or her race, colour, nationality or ethnic or national origins a person is treated less favourably than another person is or would be treated.

### Example

A job applicant is refused a post because she is black.

Direct race discrimination also occurs if workers are segregated into groups on racial grounds (ss 1(1)(a) RRA) and 1(2) RRA).

### Example

An employer will be guilty of direct race discrimination if he keeps employees of different ethnic backgrounds segregated even if he otherwise treats them the same as employees from other backgrounds.

## Indirect race discrimination

Indirect race discrimination is covered by s 1(1)(b) RRA. It occurs where an employer applies a requirement or condition which cannot be objectively justified in terms of what is required in order to actually do the job and which has a disproportionate effect or adversely affects members of a particular racial group more than members of another group.

### Example

A requirement that applicants for a clerking job must have passed A level English would have a disproportionate effect on overseas applicants for the post (who would not have that qualification or its equivalent) (s 1(1)(b) RRA).

The requirement or condition must be an absolute requirement or condition for the job. It is not enough if the requirement or condition is only a factor in the decision making process.

### Example

In *Perera* v *Civil Service Commission (No 2)* [1983] ICR 428 the Court of Appeal ruled that when considering a candidate for a particular post, the identification of factors by an employer which included work experience in the UK, was not enough to establish a claim for indirect race discrimination. The claimant had to identify a requirement or condition for the job which if not met would be an absolute bar to getting the job.

In determining the proportion of the relevant population who can comply with a particular requirement or condition, a comparison must be made between suitably qualified people of one racial group and similarly qualified people of another. It is for the claimant who is alleging indirect race discrimination to provide evidence of the comparison and this often involves the production of complex statistical information to an industrial tribunal.

## Victimisation

Victimisation is covered by s 2 RRA. Where an employer or a fellow employee ("the discriminator") treats the victim less favourably than he treats others because the discriminator knows, believes, or suspects that the victim has or intends to:

- bring proceedings under the RRA against the discriminator;

- give evidence in proceedings under the RRA against the discriminator;

- help someone else to bring proceedings under the RRA against the discriminator; or

- allege that the discriminator has contravened the RRA

the employer commits an act of discrimination by way of victimisation (s 2 RRA).

For a further discussion of "victimisation" see Chapter 17.

## Who may be liable for acts of race discrimination?

### Potential employers and employers

Potential employers can be liable where the complaint is of discrimination in relation to an advertisement or in the treatment of job candidates.

Employers, including companies, sole traders, partnerships, associations, employers organisations, employment agencies and trade unions (and with a few exceptions) the Crown, can all be liable for race discrimination.

### Employers' vicarious liability for the acts of their employees and their independent contractors

Employers can also be held vicariously liable for any discriminatory act carried out by their employees (and by independent contractors who work under a contract personally to execute any work or labour) in the course of their employment, whether or not the employer knew or approved of the offending employee's acts (s 32(1) RRA). This means that the employer will be treated as if he had carried out the offending act himself.

### Example

In *Brown* v *Newham Health Authority* COIT 1949/29 a black nurse had a query about her wages. When she telephoned the payroll office the person answering subjected her to a torrent of abuse. The Health Authority was held liable for the abuse by the payroll worker because the payroll worker had been abusive whilst carrying out an act of giving payroll advice which the employee was authorised by the Health Authority to give.

An employer has a defence to any claim arising out of a discriminatory act of an employee, if the employer can show that he took such steps as were reasonably practicable to prevent the employee from committing the act in question, or from committing such acts generally (s 32(3) RRA).

One way for employers to prevent employees from committing discriminatory acts is the implementation of an equal opportunities policy (see Appendix 1), supplemented by adequate training of supervisory staff in the application of the policy and an effective disciplinary/grievance procedure to deal with abuses of the policy.

See also Chapter 16.

## Principals and agents

A person who appoints or authorises another to be his agent with authority (which can be either express or implied) to act on his behalf will be vicariously liable for any discriminatory act carried out by his agent (s 32(2) RRA).

### Example

A recruitment agency (the agent) appointed by an employer (the principal) could make the employer liable if, with the employer's approval (whether express or implied), the agency rejected candidates because of their race. The agent may also be liable in such circumstances.

## Employees

Section 4 RRA envisages that victims of race discrimination will bring a claim against the prospective or actual employer. However, employees who discriminate against their fellow workers can be made respondents (or defendants) to claims and are often individually named as respondents (together with their employer). The right to bring proceedings against an employee or to join an employee as a co-respondent in proceedings brought against the employer arises under s 33(1) and s 33(2) RRA. These sections provide that a person who knowingly aids another to do an act which is unlawful under the RRA shall be treated as having committed the unlawful act himself.

## Partnerships

The RRA does not apply to firms with less than six partners.

Where race is a genuine occupational qualification ("GOQ" see page 16) for a position it is not unlawful for a partnership of any size to discriminate.

A prospective or existing partnership consisting of six or more partners will be subject to s 10(2) RRA which provides that partners must not discriminate:

- in the arrangements made for determining who should be offered a partnership;

- by refusing or deliberately omitting to offer a partnership;

- in the terms on which the partnership is offered;

- in giving a partner access to benefits, facilities or services;

- by refusing or deliberately omitting to offer access to benefits, facilities or services;

- by expelling a partner; or

- by subjecting a partner to any other detriment.

Thus partnerships are liable in the same way as any other employer for discriminatory acts against their employees.

## Trade unions and employers' associations

Section 11 RRA provides that it is unlawful for trade unions, employers' associations, (*e.g.* the Confederation of British Industry), and professional or trade associations to discriminate against a non-member:

- in the terms on which it is prepared to admit him to membership;

- by refusing or deliberately omitting to accept his application for membership.

It is unlawful for such organisations to discriminate against a member:

- in the way it affords him access to any benefits, facilities or services, or by refusing or deliberately omitting to afford him access to them;

- by depriving him of membership or by varying the terms on which he is a member; or

- by subjecting him to any other detriment.

## Trade union shop stewards

Shop stewards can be personally liable for race discrimination if they pressurise employers into unlawful acts of discrimination, *e.g.* by threatening to ballot for industrial action if an ethnic minority employee is selected for promotion by the employer, and the employer does not then promote the employee. In such circumstances the employer will be liable. The trade union itself may also be guilty of discrimination if when exerting pressure, the shop steward was acting with the union's authority as its agent.

## Qualifying bodies

Section 12 RRA applies to bodies which can confer an authorisation or qualification which is needed for, or facilitates engagement in, a particular trade or profession. The Law Society, British Medical Association or the British Judo Association are examples of "qualifying bodies" for the purpose of the RRA.

It is unlawful for a qualifying body to discriminate against a person:

- in the terms on which it is prepared to confer on him that authorisation or qualification;

- by refusing or deliberately omitting to grant his application for an authorisation or qualification;

- by withdrawing it from him or varying the terms on which he holds the authorisation or qualification.

### Example

In *Bolton-Mitchell* v *Common Professional Examination Board and the Council of Legal Education* [1978] IRLR 525 the "qualifying bodies" were the Board and the Council who were held to have committed an act of unlawful indirect race discrimination by imposing extra academic requirements on overseas non-law graduates in order for them to complete the academic stage of training for the Bar.

## Vocational training bodies

Vocational training bodies include government and private sector training organisations which train people for employment, *e.g.* Industrial Training Boards.

Section 13 RRA provides that it is unlawful for any person, who provides or makes arrangements for the provision of facilities for training, to discriminate against a person seeking or undergoing training which would help him gain any employment either:

- in the terms on which that person affords him access to any training course or other facilities concerned with such training;

- by refusing or deliberately omitting to afford access to training; or

- by terminating the training or by subjecting him to any detriment during the course of his training.

## Employment agencies

Section 78(1) RRA defines an "employment agency" as a person who, for profit or not, provides services for the purpose of finding employment for workers or supplying employers with workers.

### Example

In *Bramble* v *Gibbens Car Hire* COIT 809/192 a car hire firm which used self-employed drivers was held by an industrial tribunal to be an "employment agency" because it supplied the drivers to customers and thereby enabled the drivers to earn a living. This case emphasises that tribunals will interpret the law broadly in deciding whether an act of discrimination has taken place.

It is unlawful for an employment agency to discriminate:

- in the terms on which it offers to provide any of its services;

- by refusing or deliberately omitting to provide any of its service;

- in the way it provides its services.

An employment agency shall not be liable if:

- it proves that it acted in reliance on a statement made to it by the principal that its action in recruiting or supplying staff would not be unlawful; and

- it was reasonable for the agency to rely on the principal's statement.

# Who can complain of race discrimination?

## Job applicants and employees

Any person who is a victim of any of the acts of unlawful discrimination outlined above can bring a complaint to an industrial tribunal alleging race discrimination. The right to complain will extend to job applicants, employees, (*i.e.* those who have entered into or who work under a contract of employment or apprenticeship), and also self employed persons who do some or all of the work themselves, rather than employing others to carry out work on their behalf.

## Contract workers

A "contract worker" is a person employed by one individual and who is supplied by that individual under a contract to work for another person (the "principal"). A typical example is a temporary secretary supplied by an employment agency. s 7 RRA provides protection for contract workers in respect of race discrimination.

It is often a surprise to the principal who uses temporary staff supplied by an agency, to find that he can be liable for acts of discrimination perpetrated against workers supplied by an agency.

The principal must not discriminate against contract workers on the grounds of race in respect of:

- the terms on which he allows him to do the work;

- by not allowing him to work or continue to work;

- the way he affords him access to any benefits, facilities or services, or by refusing or deliberately omitting to afford him access to them;

- by subjecting him to any other detriment.

It is not unlawful for the principal to discriminate in favour of a non-British resident by training him in skills which the worker intends to exercise wholly outside Britain (s 7(4) RRA)

## The armed forces

Serving members of the armed forces are protected from acts of race discrimination by s 75(2)(c) RRA, but the protection does not extend to recruitment. Complainants from the armed forces must follow an internal procedure rather than the industrial tribunal procedure (s 75(2) RRA).

## The police

Section 16 RRA provides that a police officer, cadet, or special constable, or a person applying to join the police force has the same rights as an ordinary employee. The employer for these purposes is the Chief Officer of Police or the local police authority. Sums awarded by way of compensation and any costs or expenses incurred by the police through liability for race discrimination are payable out of the police fund.

# Lawful race discrimination, defences and exemptions

## Statutory exemptions

The RRA does not apply to holders of a "statutory office" (s 75(10)(c) RRA) including government ministers and Justices of the Peace.

Employees in private households such as gardeners, nannies and cleaners are not protected save in respect of discrimination by way of victimisation (s 2 RRA).

See also Chapter 27.

## Justification

Section 1(1)(b)(ii) RRA provides that in the context of indirect race discrimination a racially discriminatory requirement or condition imposed by an employer may be justified and, if it can be, it will not be unlawful. It is for the employer or the person imposing the requirement or condition to show that it was justified irrespective of the colour, race, nationality or ethnic or national origins of the person to whom it is applied (*Mandla* v *Lee* [1983] IRLR 209).

### Examples

In *Hampson* v *Department of Education* [1989] IRLR 69 the Court of Appeal decided that the test of justification was an objective one. There had to be an objective balance between the discriminatory effect of the condition and the reasonable needs of the particular employer. It is not sufficient for the employer to establish that he considered his reason for imposing the requirement or condition to be adequate. In the Hampson case, Lord Justice Balcombe referred to the House of Lords decision in *Rainey* v *Greater Glasgow Health Board* [1987] IRLR 26 in which the House of Lords, applying the decision of the ECJ in *Bilka Kaufhaus GmbH* v *Weber von Hartz* [1987] IRLR 317 ruled that to justify imposing a condition that might otherwise be discriminatory an employer had to show that the requirement met a real need of the business, which need could be objectively justified. The need might be economic, or linked to administrative efficiency.

In *Ojutiku* v *Manpower Services Commission* [1982] ICR 661 the applicants were denied sponsorship for management training because they lacked management experience. The industrial tribunal decided that this requirement was indirectly discriminatory because "coloured" people have a lesser chance than white people of gaining management experience in industry. The Court of Appeal overruled the industrial tribunal and decided that the requirement for "management experience" was justifiable and would be thought to be so by "right thinking people".

## Genuine occupational qualification ("the GOQ exception")

Section 5 RRA provides that it is not unlawful to refuse to employ, or to offer employment to, an individual from a particular race where being from a particular racial group is a genuine occupational qualification for the job, *e.g.* to produce authenticity in a dramatic production or work of art. The GOQ exception will also apply where a worker is required to provide persons of a particular racial group with personal services promoting their welfare which can be most effectively provided by someone from the same racial group.

### Example

In *Tottenham Green Under Five Centre* v *Marshall* [1989] IRLR 147 the EAT decided that it was not unlawful race discrimination for the Centre to advertise for an "Afro-Caribbean worker" in order to maintain a racial mix of staff to deal with a racially mixed group of children. The worker was required to provide "personal services" to promote the welfare of the group.

An example of where the GOQ exception did not apply was where a local authority advertised for Afro-Caribbean or Asian applicants to apply for jobs in the Housing Benefits Department. The advertisement was unlawful because the jobs were at managerial level and the post-holders would not have close contact with Afro-Caribbeans or Asians as part of their job.

Generally, the GOQ exception will be restrictively interpreted by industrial tribunals as it provides an exception to what would otherwise be race discrimination. In exercising their judgment, tribunals should take a broad commonsense approach.

The GOQ exception will not apply where the employer already has employees from a racial group who are capable of carrying out those duties.

## Training in skills to be exercised outside Great Britain

This is covered by ss 6 and 7(4) RRA. It is not unlawful for employers to discriminate positively in order to benefit a person who is not ordinarily resident in Great Britain where the objective is to train the person in skills which it appears to the employer that person intends to use wholly outside Great Britain.

## Seamen recruited abroad

With the exception of those covered by the Race Relations (Offshore Employment) Order 1987 (SI 1987/929) (page 4), seamen who are recruited overseas, even if they are brought to Great Britain, are excluded from protection under the RRA.

## Positive discrimination

Whilst, in general, preferential treatment of any racial group is unlawful, the RRA does allow certain limited forms of positive discrimination. For example, s 35 RRA allows for discrimination in favour of members of a particular racial group who have "special needs" in regard to their education, training or welfare.

## Summary
## Race Discrimination

- The principal statute is the Race Relations Act 1976 ("RRA").

- There are three forms of race discrimination: direct race discrimination, indirect race discrimination and victimisation.

- Employers and potential employers, employees, partnerships (with more than six partners), the self-employed, trade unions, shop stewards, employers associations, employment agencies and (with limited exceptions) the Crown can all be liable for acts of race discrimination.

- The above can be liable for discriminating on the ground of colour, race, nationality, or ethnic or national origins, in recruitment, promotion, training, working conditions and dismissal.

- Compensation for race discrimination is unlimited and compensation can carry interest.

- Potential employees, employees, the self-employed and workers provided by an agency can all bring complaints of race discrimination to an industrial tribunal. There is no requirement that complainants should have 2 years' service to bring a complaint.

- There are limited exceptions where race discrimination is permitted, *e.g.* where being from a particular racial group is a "genuine occupational qualification" for the job.

# CONTENTS OF CHAPTER 2

## Sex Discrimination

# 2. SEX DISCRIMINATION

## Relevant law

### Acts of Parliament

*Sex Discrimination Act 1975*

The principal statute is the SDA which applies to the whole of Great Britain but not to Northern Ireland. The SDA enables individuals to bring claims for unlawful sex discrimination in industrial tribunals against their employer, co-workers and others. The SDA has been amended by the Sex Discrimination Act 1986, the Employment Act 1989 and the Trade Union Reform and Employment Rights Act 1993 to bring it more closely into line with European Community Law, but the majority of its provisions remain unchanged.

### Statutory instruments

*Sex Discrimination and Equal Pay (Remedies) Regulations 1993 (SI 1993/2798)*

These regulations provide that, as from 23 November 1993, industrial tribunals have the power to award unlimited compensation to victims of sex discrimination and to award simple interest on awards for arrears of remuneration.

*Sex Discrimination and Equal Pay (Miscellaneous Amendments) Regulations 1996 (SI 1996/438)*

These regulations, which came into force on 25 March 1996, enable an industrial tribunal to award compensation to a person who has suffered indirect sex discrimination even where the respondent did not intend to discriminate.

## European Community law

### Treaty of Rome

The Treaty of Rome is the basis for European Community law as a whole. Article 119 of the Treaty sets out the principle that men and women should receive equal pay for equal work (see Chapter 14).

### The Equal Treatment Directive 76/207/EEC ("The ET Directive")

This lays down in European Union Law the principle of equal treatment for men and women in respect of working conditions and access to vocational training, promotion and dismissal (see Chapter 14).

## Codes of practice

### The Equal Opportunities Commission Statutory Code of Practice

The Equal Opportunities Commission ("EOC") is a statutory body established under the SDA to promote sex equality and to enforce the SDA. In 1985 the EOC issued a code of practice for the elimination of discrimination on the grounds of sex and marriage and the promotion of equality of opportunity in employment. The EOC code gives practical guidance on the provisions of the SDA. Whilst the EOC code does not impose legal obligations its provisions are far-reaching, because an industrial tribunal must take any relevant paragraph in the EOC code into account in deciding any question of sex discrimination.

### European Commission Recommendation on the Protection of the Dignity of Women and Men at Work and Code of Practice on Measures to Combat Sexual Harassment ("EC Code of Practice")

The EC Code of Practice was adopted by the European Commission in November 1991. Although it is not legally binding and does not itself give rise to legal rights and liabilities, courts and industrial tribunals may take it into account in determining whether particular conduct amounts to sexual harassment.

## The forms of sex discrimination

The SDA prohibits the following forms of discrimination:

- direct sex discrimination;
- indirect sex discrimination;
- direct marital discrimination;
- indirect marital discrimination; and
- victimisation.

### Discrimination against men

Whilst references in the SDA (and, for simplicity, most of the references in this book) are to discrimination against women, it is important to remember that, in almost all circumstances, the SDA has equal application to discrimination against men (s 2(1) SDA). Exceptions include matters which relate to pregnancy and childbirth, when women can lawfully be treated more favourably than men.

### Direct sex discrimination

This is governed by s 1(1)(a) SDA and occurs where a woman is treated less favourably than a man is or would have been treated and the difference in treatment is due to her sex.

### Example

A job applicant is refused a post because she is a woman, when a man with the same abilities would have been successful.

To establish direct sex discrimination, the woman does not have to compare her treatment with that of an actual man; a comparison with a hypothetical man will suffice.

> **Example**
>
> A woman is the only qualified candidate for a job, but the employer decides not to employ her because she would be the only woman in an otherwise all male team. Although there is no actual male candidate, the woman could argue that a man in her position would have been successful.

In determining whether the treatment of the woman is or would be different to the treatment of a man, the comparison must be such that the relevant circumstances of each case are the same or not materially different (s 5(3) SDA). In other words, like must be compared with like.

This means that the hypothetical male candidate in the above example above must have all the same attributes and abilities as the woman, and the question to be asked is whether such a man would have been given the job in the same all-male team. The employer cannot argue in his defence that the man would not have been given the job in an all-female team (*Greig* v *Community Industry & Ahern* [1979] IRLR 158).

Even if the employer has other reasons for the difference in treatment, there will still be direct sex discrimination if sex is the substantial factor in the employer's decision. (*Owen & Briggs* v *James* [1982] IRLR 502).

## Indirect sex discrimination

This is covered by s 1(1)(b) SDA, and occurs where all of the following conditions are met:

- a requirement or condition is applied to a woman which is or would be applied equally to a man;

- the proportion of women who can comply with the requirement or condition is considerably smaller than the proportion of men who can comply;

- the requirement or condition is not justifiable on non-sex grounds; and

- the woman suffers a detriment because she cannot comply with the requirement or condition.

## Example

A full-time employee of the Home Office with two young children applied to work part time. The Home Office refused the application because it had a general policy that part-time working would not be allowed at the employee's grade. The EAT decided that there was a requirement to work full-time, and that the proportion of women who could comply with the requirement was considerably smaller than the proportion of men who could comply because of women's family commitments. The requirement could not be justified in this case, and therefore the Home Office's refusal was indirect sex discrimination (*Home Office* v *Holmes* [1984] ICR 678).

If a requirement or condition is imposed on men and women because a considerably smaller proportion of women will be able to comply, such action is likely to be direct sex discrimination because a woman is being treated less favourably because of her sex.

## Example

An employer would rather employ men than women to do tele-sales work because he thinks that female employees may want to take maternity leave. He imposes a requirement that all applicants must be over 6 feet tall, knowing that a significantly smaller proportion of women than men will be able to comply. This is direct sex discrimination.

There are circumstances in which a particular requirement or condition may be justified, thereby rendering it lawful. To establish justification, the employer must show that the requirement or condition:

- corresponds to a real need of the business or undertaking;
- is appropriate with a view to achieving the employer's objective; and
- is necessary to that end.

(*Bilka-Kaufhaus GmbH* v *Weber Von Hartz* [1987] IRLR 317).

Therefore requirements and conditions which are only imposed for the employer's convenience will not be justifiable.

## Direct marital discrimination

This is covered by s 3(1)(a) SDA, and occurs where a married person of either sex is treated less favourably than an unmarried person of the same sex; and the difference in treatment is due to the fact that he or she is married.

> **Example**
>
> An employer refuses a job application by a married woman and gives the job to a lesser qualified unmarried woman. The employer tells the first applicant that a married woman's place is in the home. This is direct marital discrimination.

The SDA does not prohibit less favourable treatment of an unmarried person on the grounds of marital status.

A married person is only protected against marital discrimination if he or she was married at the time of the discriminatory act. Therefore less favourable treatment due to an intention to get married does not fall within the SDA.

If a married woman is treated less favourably than an unmarried man, her claim would be based on direct sex discrimination rather than marital discrimination.

> **Example**
>
> If, in the first example above, the job was given to an unmarried man, the married woman could claim direct sex discrimination as the employer would not have made a similar remark to a married man. The treatment is on the grounds of the woman's sex.

## Indirect marital discrimination

This is covered by s 3(1)(b) SDA, and occurs where all of the following conditions are met:

- a requirement or condition is applied to a married person which is or would be applied equally to an unmarried person;

- the proportion of married people who can comply with the requirement or condition is considerably smaller than the proportion of unmarried people of the same sex who can comply;

- the requirement or condition is not justifiable;

- the married person suffers a detriment because he or she cannot comply with the requirement or condition.

## Victimisation

Victimisation is covered by s 4(1) SDA, and occurs where the following conditions are met:

- the discriminator treats the victim less favourably that he treats or would treat another person in like circumstances; and

- the reason for the difference in treatment is that the victim has done, or the discriminator knows or suspects that the victim is about to do, one of the following:

  - bring proceedings under the SDA or the Equal Pay Act 1970 ("EqPA") (see Chapter 14) against the discriminator or any other person

  - give evidence in proceedings under the SDA or EqPA against the discriminator or any other person

  - help someone else to bring proceedings under the SDA or EqPA against the discriminator or any other person

  - allege that the discriminator or any other person has committed an act which contravened the SDA or EqPA.

---

**Example**

A woman brings a claim against her employer for equal pay under EqPA. The claim fails but the employer demotes the woman for having pursued her claim. The employer's conduct amounts to victimisation.

---

Section 4(1) SDA covers actions by the victim against the discriminator or "any other person".

---

**Example**

A woman gives evidence against her old employer in proceedings brought by her friend under the SDA. The woman's old employer and new employer exchange information and the woman is denied promotion by her new employer because of her actions. The new employer's conduct will amount to victimisation.

---

The provisions do not apply to the treatment of a woman due to allegations by her which were false and which were not made in good faith (s 4(2) SDA).

For a further discussion of "victimisation" see Chapter 17.

## Who may be liable for acts of sex discrimination?

*Potential employers and employers*

Employers including companies, sole traders, partnerships, associations, employment agencies and trade unions and, with a few exceptions, the Crown can all be liable for acts of sex discrimination. Potential employers can be liable for sex discrimination where the complaint is of discrimination in relation to an advertisement or the treatment of job candidates.

## Employers' vicarious liability for acts of employees and independent contractors

Employers will be vicariously liable for any discriminatory act done by their employees (and by independent contractors who work under a contract personally to execute any work or labour) in the course of the employee's employment, whether or not the employer knew or approved of the offending employee's acts (s 41(1) SDA).

### Example

In *Brownhill* v *Gateway Foodmarkets* SCOIT S/3968/90 Ms Brownhill was sexually harassed by her manger, who had commented on the size of her breasts; said what he would like to do with her body; and had pretended to pull his trouser-zip down when the two of them had been alone. The tribunal ruled that the employer was vicariously liable under the SDA for the manager's conduct because whilst he was at work and whilst he was meant to be responsible for managing Ms Brownhill, the manager had harassed her.

See also Chapter 16.

## Principals and agents

A person who appoints and authorises another to be his agent with authority (either express or implied) to act on his behalf may become vicariously liable for any discriminatory act carried out by the agent, *i.e.* anything done by the agent with the principal's authority will be treated as having been done by the principal as well as by the agent, thereby making the principal and agent liable (s 41(2) SDA).

### Example

A recruitment agency ("the agent") appointed by an employer ("the principal") could make the employer liable if when recruiting staff for the employer, the agency selected candidates because of their sex. The agent could also be liable if he followed the employer's instruction to recruit or not to recruit candidates because of their sex unless a "GOQ" exception applies.

## Employees

In practice, although employees are rarely made liable for their acts of discrimination, they are often individually named as respondents in claims for victimisation of another employee together with their employer.

## Partnerships

Unlike s 10(2) RRA (see Chapter 1), following amendment by the Sex Discrimination Act 1986, the SDA does apply to partnerships with less than six partners.

Partnerships are liable in the same way as any other employer for discriminatory acts against their employees.

Where the partners themselves are not employees, they have effectively the same rights against the firm and their partners as employees by virtue of s 11 SDA.

This provides that partners must not discriminate:

- in the arrangements made for determining who should be offered a partnership;

- by refusing or deliberately omitting to offer a partnership or in the terms on which the partnership is offered;

- in giving a partner access to benefits, facilities or services;

- by refusing or deliberately omitting access to benefits, facilities or services;

- by expelling a partner, or by subjecting a partner to any other detriment.

## Trade unions and employers' associations

Section 12 SDA provides that it is unlawful for trade unions and employers' associations (*e.g.* the Confederation of British Industry), and professional or trade associations to discriminate against a non-member:

- in the terms on which it is prepared to admit her to membership; or

- by refusing or deliberately omitting to accept her application for membership.

It is also unlawful for such organisations to discriminate against a member:

- in the way in which it affords her access to any benefits, facilities or services, or by refusing or deliberately omitting to afford her access to them;

- by depriving her of membership or varying the terms on which she is a member; or

- by subjecting her to any other detriment.

Section 77 SDA and s 6 Sex Discrimination Act 1986 also provide that the terms of collective agreements and the rules of trade unions and employers' associations which purport to discriminate on grounds of sex or marital status are void and unenforceable.

Sections 48 and 49(1) SDA give these organisations a limited right to discriminate positively in favour of either sex in relation to training members, encouraging them to take advantage of opportunities for holding a particular post, encouraging non-members to join, and by reserving seats on their elected bodies where this is necessary to secure a reasonable minimum number of that sex to serve on the body in question.

## Qualifying bodies

Section 13 SDA applies to bodies which can confer an authorisation or qualification which is needed for, or facilitates engagement in, a particular trade or profession. The Institute of Chartered Accountants and the Law Society are examples of qualifying bodies.

It is unlawful for a qualifying body to discriminate against a person:

- in the terms on which it is prepared to confer on her that authorisation or qualification;

- by refusing or deliberately omitting to grant her application for an authorisation or qualification;

- by withdrawing it from her or varying the terms on which she holds the authorisation or qualification.

Section 6 Sex Discrimination Act 1986 provides that any rule made by a qualifying body which purports to discriminate on grounds of sex or marital status is void and unenforceable.

## Vocational training bodies

The term "vocational training bodies" includes both governmental and private sector organisations which provide training to help people find employment, *e.g.* Industrial Training Boards. Section 14 SDA provides that it is unlawful for any person who provides, arranges or facilitates training to discriminate against a person seeking or undergoing training which would help to prepare her for any employment, either:

- in the terms on which access to any training course or other facilities concerned with such training is offered;

- by refusing or deliberately omitting to offer such access;

- by terminating her training or by subjecting her to any detriment during the course of such training.

## Employment agencies

Section 82(1) SDA defines an "employment agency" as a person or organisation who, whether for profit or not, provides services for the purpose of finding employment for workers or who supplies employers with workers. Such services may include guidance on careers and any other services related to employment (s 15(3) SDA). Local (or other) educational authorities who provide employment services may be liable for sex discrimination under s 15(2) SDA.

It is unlawful for an employment agency to discriminate:

- in the terms on which it offers to provide any of its services;

- by refusing or deliberately omitting to provide any of its services;

- in the way it provides its services.

It is not unlawful for an employment agency to discriminate if the discrimination only concerns employment which the employer could lawfully refuse to offer (s 15(4) SDA).

   An employment agency is not liable if it proves that it acted in reliance on a statement made to it by the employer that, due to the operation of s 15(4) SDA, its action would not be unlawful, and it was reasonable for the agency to rely on the employer's statement.

## Who can complain of sex discrimination?

### Job applicants and employees

Any person who is a victim of any of the acts of unlawful discrimination outlined above can bring a complaint to an industrial tribunal alleging sex discrimination. The right to complain will extend to job applicants, employees (*i.e.* those who have entered into or who work under a contract of employment or apprenticeship), and also self-employed persons who do some, or all of the work themselves rather than employing others to carry out work on their behalf.

### Contract workers

A contract worker is a person employed by one individual (*e.g.* an employment agency) and who is supplied by that individual under a contract to work for another person (the "principal"). Section 9 SDA provides protection from discrimination for contract workers.

   A contract worker is protected under the SDA against her employer in the same way as any other employee. She also has specific protection against discrimination by her principal in respect of:

- the terms on which he allows her to do the work;

- not being allowed to do or continue to do the work;

- the way in which he affords her access to any benefits, facilities or services or by refusing or deliberately omitting to provide access to them;
- being subjected to any other detriment.

> **Example**
>
> Where a principal would not allow a woman to return to work after taking maternity leave, the principal was liable for sex discrimination (*BP Chemicals Ltd* v *Gillick* [1995] IRLR 128).

It is not unlawful for a principal to prevent a contract worker doing work if the work is such that being of the opposite sex would be a GOQ. The employment agency itself does not breach the SDA if the discrimination only concerns employment which the principal could lawfully refuse to offer (s 15(4) SDA), *e.g.* where a GOQ applies.

An employment agency is not liable if it proves that it acted in reliance on a statement made to it by the principal to the effect that, by reason of the operation of s 15(4) SDA, its actions would not be unlawful, and it was reasonable for the agency to rely on the principal's statement.

## The self-employed

Although they do not qualify for many other statutory rights, *e.g.* the right to claim unfair dismissal or a redundancy payment, many people who are self-employed have the same protection under the SDA as employees.

The SDA covers employment "under a contract personally to execute any work or labour" – (s 82(1) SDA). Provided a self-employed person works for another under a contract made between them, and the main purpose of that contract is the carrying out of the work by the self-employed individual personally, then that individual will be protected against any discriminatory acts of the person for whom the work is being done (*BP Chemicals Ltd* v *Gillick* [1995] IRLR 128).

> **Example**
>
> A woman has a contract with a company to clean its offices. She decides to take a holiday, and her sister takes her place as a favour to her. As the sister has no contract with the company, she does not come within s 82(1) SDA, and therefore has no protection against discriminatory acts by the employer.

## The armed forces

Members of the armed forces were previously excluded from the protection of the SDA by virtue of s 85(4) SDA.

Until 1991, the Ministry of Defence operated a discriminatory policy of dismissing service women who became pregnant. Such women could not pursue claims under the SDA, but in 1991 the MOD conceded that its policy was in breach of the ET Directive. A number of high profile claims were subsequently made under the ET Directive by servicewomen who had been discharged from the armed forces under this policy.

Since February 1995 the Sex Discrimination Act 1975 (Application to Armed Forces etc) Regulations 1994 have given members of the armed forces protection under the SDA against sex discrimination, except where discrimination is necessary to ensure "combat effectiveness". (See also Chapter 26).

## The police

Section 17 SDA provides that a police officer, cadet or special constable, or a person applying to join the police force, has the same rights as an ordinary employee. The employer in this case is the Chief Officer of Police or the local police authority. Any sums paid by way of compensation and any costs or expenses incurred through liability for sex discrimination by the police are payable out of the police fund.

## Lawful sex discrimination, defences and exemptions

### Statutory exemptions

The SDA does not apply to the holder of a "statutory office", *e.g.* Justices of the Peace or ministers of the Crown (s 85(2) and s 85(10) SDA). (See also Chapter 27.)

### Genuine occupational qualification ("the GOQ exception")

Section 7 SDA provides that discrimination may be lawful where being of a particular sex is a GOQ for the job.

---

**Example**

A employer could insist on recruiting only a man to illustrate the performance of its new razor in a television commercial.

---

Where there is a GOQ, the employer may only discriminate:

- in the arrangements made for recruiting for the job;
- by refusing or deliberately omitting to offer the job;
- in the way in which the worker is afforded access to opportunities for promotion, for transfer to or for training for the job, or by requiring or deliberately omitting to offer such opportunities.

These are the only circumstances where a GOQ may be relied upon. An employer cannot argue a GOQ defence when he discriminates against a woman in her existing job by, *e.g.* denying her access to benefits or dismissing her.

A GOQ defence can only be applied to sex, and not marital, discrimination.

A further limitation on the GOQ defence applies where the employer already has a sufficient number of male or female employees who are capable of carrying out the duties within the vacant post, and it would not be unduly inconvenient for the employer to employ them on those duties.

## Example

A man applies for a job as a sales assistant in a women's clothes shop. The shop refuses to employ him on the basis that customers will want to have their bust measurements taken, and a woman is required to preserve decency and privacy. However, as the shop already employs a large number of female sales assistants who can perform the task when needed without inconvenience, there is no GOQ defence (*Etam plc* v *Rowan* [1989] IRLR 150).

Section 7(2), SDA (as amended by the Sex Discrimination Act 1986), sets out an exhaustive list of GOQs which may be relied upon in defence to a claim of discrimination. A reason which cannot be fitted into any of the categories will not be a valid defence. The list of GOQs is as follows:

- for reasons of physiology or authenticity;

- to preserve decency or privacy;

- where only single-sex accommodation is available;

- due to the nature of the establishment;

- where personal welfare and educational services are provided;

- due to the laws or customs of a country outside the United Kingdom;

- where a married couple is required.

*Physiology and authenticity as a GOQ*

This is covered by s 7(2)(a) SDA. Physiology can be relied on as a GOQ where only one sex is physically capable of doing a particular job, or where only one sex is appropriate, *e.g.* a model for ladies' underwear. Physiology expressly excludes strength and stamina. This does not mean that employers cannot require these attributes in an employee, but they must not assume that only men will have them.

## Example

An employer who advertises for a man for heavy labouring work cannot rely on a GOQ defence against a claim for sex discrimination.

There will be a GOQ if only one sex will provide authenticity in dramatic performances or other entertainment.

---

### Example

An advertisement for a woman to play the part of Juliet in a production of "Romeo and Juliet" will not be discriminatory.

---

*Decency or privacy*

This is covered by s 7(2)(b) SDA. There will only be a GOQ under this category if a job needs to be done by one particular sex to preserve decency or privacy because:

● the job is likely to involve physical contact with men or women in circumstances where they might reasonably object to the job being carried out by someone of the opposite sex; or

● the holder of the job is likely to work in circumstances where members of one sex are in a state of undress or are using sanitary facilities and therefore might reasonably object to the presence of the opposite sex; or

● the job holder is likely, as part of the job, to have to work or live in a private home and objection might reasonably be taken to allowing a man or woman either:

    –    the degree of physical or social contact with a person living in the home; or

    –    the knowledge of intimate details of such a person's life which the job is likely to entail.

To establish a GOQ it must be necessary, rather than merely preferable, for only one sex to perform the job. In particular employers cannot rely on customer or client pressure in discriminating against one sex.

## Example

A general medical practice, the majority of whose patients would rather see a female doctor, will not have a GOQ defence if it only advertises for a woman doctor. The recruitment of a woman may be preferable to the practice, but it is not necessary.

The job does not have to have a direct connection with circumstances where decency or privacy may need to be preserved for there to be a GOQ. It is sufficient for the requirement for decency or privacy to be reasonably incidental to the job.

## Example

An employer could assert a decency and privacy defence where female employees tended to strip to their underwear during rest periods. Although undressing was not necessary as part of the job, it was a necessary part of resting and was therefore reasonably incidental to the job (*Sisley* v *Britannia Security Systems Ltd* [1983] ICR 628).

*Single sex accommodation*

This is covered by s 7(2)(c) SDA. This GOQ defence may apply where, due to the nature or location of the establishment, it is impracticable for the worker to live elsewhere than in the premises provided by the employer.

The employer has to show that:

• the only available premises for the job are lived in by members of only one sex and there are no separate sleeping and sanitary facilities that can be used in privacy by members of the other sex; and

• it is not reasonable to expect the employer either to equip the premises with separate sleeping accommodation and sanitary facilities or to provide alternative premises for members of the other sex.

Employees only "live in" the premises if they have temporary or permanent residence there. They do not "live in" if they merely rest there between shifts and later go home.

Whether it is reasonable for the employer to alter the premises, or to provide alternative accommodation, depends on the circumstances of each case. The cost of making special arrangements will be an important factor in determining reasonableness, and employers trying to rely on this GOQ defence in industrial tribunal proceedings should have details of the likely cost of making the arrangements to support their case.

*Nature of the establishment*

Section 7(2)(d) SDA covers single-sex establishments such as hospitals, prisons, children's and nursing homes where it is impracticable to employ persons of a particular sex. To qualify, the following conditions must be met:

- it must be a hospital, prison or other establishment for persons requiring special care, supervision and attention; and

- those persons are all of one sex (disregarding any persons whose presence is exceptional); and

- it is reasonable, having regard to the essential character of the establishment, that the job should not be held by a person of the opposite sex.

The whole establishment does not have to be entirely for one sex, provided the employee is to work exclusively in one part which satisfies all of the conditions, *e.g.* an all-female wing in a special secure hospital.

*Provision of personal welfare and educational services*

This is covered by s 7(2)(e) SDA. An employer can rely on this GOQ when the worker provides individuals with personal services promoting their welfare or education, or similar personal services, and those services can most effectively be provided by one particular sex.

### Example

A rape victim support unit may have a GOQ defence if it recruits only women to provide counselling.

(Note: s 7(2)(f) SDA has been repealed.)

*Employment outside the UK*

This is covered by s 7(2)(g) SDA. An employer can establish a GOQ if the job is likely to involve the performance of duties outside the United Kingdom in a country whose laws or customs are such that the duties could not, or could not effectively, be performed by a woman, *e.g.* jobs in certain Middle Eastern countries.

*Married couples*

This is covered by s 7(2)(h) SDA. Where the job is one of two to be held by a married couple, the employer is not liable under the SDA if he rejects applicants from two men, two women or a man and a woman who are not married.

*Charities*

Provisions contained in enactments or instruments of charitable trusts, which confer benefits on members of one sex only, are not unlawful by virtue of s 43 SDA.

## Other exemptions

*Sport*

By virtue of s 44 SDA it is lawful to discriminate against male or female competitors by not allowing them to participate in sports, games or other activities of a competitive nature, where the physical strength, stamina or physique of the average woman puts her at a disadvantage to the average man.

This exception only applies to sports where strength, stamina and physique are important, *e.g.* rugby, but not chess.

The exception does not apply to people who participate in the sport but not as competitors, *e.g.* a referee or scorer (*British Judo Association* v *Petty* [1981] IRLR 484).

*Communal accommodation*

This is covered by s 46 SDA. The term "communal accommodation" means residential accommodation and includes dormitories or other shared sleeping accommodation which, for reasons of privacy or decency, should be used by members of one sex only. It also includes residential accommodation which should be used by one sex only because of the nature of its sanitary facilities.

Where an employer provides communal accommodation to one sex only on grounds of privacy and decency, employees of the other sex have no claim for discrimination provided that the accommodation is managed in such a way as to be as fair as possible to both men and women.

If the employer can discriminate in admission to communal accommodation, he can also discriminate in the provision of benefits, facilities or services which can only be provided to those using the communal accommodation.

The employer will only have a defence to claims by disadvantaged employees if he arranges, as far as is reasonably practicable, to compensate those employees for the detriment caused by the discrimination.

### Example

A employer whose employees are almost all men and who provides only male residential accommodation will not be liable if it makes a compensatory payment to the female staff in lieu of the residential accommodation.

This exception can be distinguished from the GOQ of single sex accommodation (above). That GOQ applies where an employee is prevented from doing a job because she cannot use the communal accommodation or sanitary facilities. The exception under s 46 SDA applies where the employee is able to do the job but suffers a disadvantage by not being able to use the accommodation or facilities and is compensated by her employer as a result.

## Summary
## Sex Discrimination

- The principal statute is the Sex Discrimination Act 1975 (SDA) which applies to men and women.

- There are 5 forms of sex discrimination: direct sex discrimination, indirect sex discrimination, direct marital discrimination, indirect marital discrimination and victimisation.

- Complaints of sex discrimination are made to an industrial tribunal.

- Employers, potential employers, the self-employed, partnerships, trade unions, employers' associations, employment agencies and employees can all be liable for acts of sex discrimination.

- Compensation for sex discrimination is unlimited.

- Potential employees, employees, the self-employed and workers provided by an employment agency can all bring complaints of sex discrimination to an industrial tribunal. There is no requirement that complainants should have 2 years' service before bringing a complaint.

- There are limited exceptions where sex discrimination is permitted.

# CONTENTS OF CHAPTER 3

## Disability Discrimination

# 3. DISABILITY DISCRIMINATION

## Relevant law

### Acts of Parliament

*The Disabled Persons (Employment) Acts 1944 and 1958*

Until 2 December 1996 (the date on which most of the provisions relating to employment in the Disability Discrimination Act 1995 (DDA) came into force (see below)), the legal requirements regarding the employment of people with disabilities will remain governed by the Disabled Persons (Employment) Acts 1944 and 1958. These Acts established a voluntary register of people with disabilities and placed certain duties and obligations on employers with 20 or more workers relating to the employment of people with disabilities who were registered under the Acts. In particular employers with 20 or more workers had to employ a quota of 3 per cent of the workforce who were disabled workers registered under the Acts. Since 2 December 1996 the registration and quota requirements no longer apply, although Schedule 1 paragraph 7(1) DDA provides that those who are registered disabled on 12 January 1995 will continue to be treated as disabled for the purposes of the DDA.

*The Companies Act 1985*

This Act requires companies employing more than 250 people to include in the Director's Report each year a policy statement concerning the employment of people with disabilities.

*The Disability Discrimination Act 1995 (DDA)*

Although the DDA received Royal Assent on 8 November 1995, most of the provisions relating to employment came into force on 2 December 1996. The DDA applies to the whole of the United Kingdom including Northern Ireland and it introduces the right for disabled people not to be discriminated against when applying for employment or during employment on the grounds of their disability.

The DDA only provides the general framework of the law and most of the detail will be contained in regulations, some of which were published in 1996 and more are expected in 1997. The DDA is complex; it includes eight schedules and there are proposals for up to 140 regulations. Readers will need to check with their solicitor or other advisor concerning the progress of regulations under the DDA. The Employers' Forum on Disability (see Appendix 4) has been established by a group of employers to provide information and to help employers to see the benefits of recruiting, retaining and developing disabled workers. Whilst the DDA introduces a whole new area of discrimination, many disabled persons groups feel that it does not go far enough to protect their rights.

## Disability discrimination outside of employment

Whilst this book deals primarily with discrimination in the context of the employer/employee relationship, the DDA also brings in new laws outlawing discrimination on the ground of disability in:

- the supply of goods, facilities and services (ss 19–21 DDA);
- the buying or renting land or property (ss 22–24 DDA);
- education (s 29 DDA);
- the provision of public transport (Part V DDA).

For further information on disability discrimination outside the employment context readers should contact their solicitor or other advisor or the NDC, NIDC or DOE (see Appendix 4).

## Disability discrimination and employment

### Which employers are not covered by the DDA?

Section 7 DDA provides that the DDA does not apply to businesses employing less than 20 employees. The number of employees employed by the employer will be considered at the date of the discriminatory act and will include part-time and temporary workers as well as employees at different establishments of the same employer. However, employees of "associated companies" such as holding companies or subsidiaries will not be included in the calculation. It would appear that whether or not a particular employer is covered by the DDA could vary from time to time.

Furthermore, the DDA does not apply to:

- independent franchise holders who employ fewer than 20 people, even if the franchise network as a whole has more than 20 employees;

- employers who employ workers on board ships, hovercraft or aeroplanes;
- the British Transport Police;
- prison officers;
- the Fire Brigade;
- the armed forces;
- charities that help people with certain kinds of disability may still discriminate positively in favour of those people in their employment policies.

## Which employers are covered by the DDA?

The DDA covers employers with more than 20 employees. For the purposes of the DDA "employers" include: companies, sole traders, partnerships, associations, employers' organisations, employment agencies, trade unions and the Crown.

## Who is a disabled person under the DDA?

Section 1 DDA defines "disability" as a "physical or mental impairment which has a substantial and long term adverse effect on [a person's] ability to carry out normal day-to-day activities". Guidance on the meaning of disability is contained in a document entitled "Guidance on matters to be taken into account in determining the Meaning of Disability Regulations 1996", published by the Department for Education and Employment (DOE). Schedule 1 to the DDA expands upon this definition which can be broken into its constituent parts as follows:

## Physical impairment

The term "physical impairment" includes impairments affecting the senses, such as sight and hearing. Furthermore, persons with a severe disfigurement will be protected under the DDA unless their disfigurement was deliberately acquired, *e.g.* tattoos and body piercing are not physical impairments under the DDA. On the other hand, someone who had plastic surgery after a severe accident would be treated as disabled under the DDA, even-though their disfigurement did not affect their ability to carry out normal day-to-day activities.

## Mental impairment

A mental impairment will include learning disabilities as well as clinically well recognised mental illnesses. Certain conditions which are listed in the Meaning of Disability Regulations are not regarded as impairment for the purposes of the DDA. These conditions include personality disorders such as kleptomania, pyromania and other psychopathic disorders will not be mental impairments under the DDA.

## Drug dependency

Dependency on alcohol, tobacco and other drugs do not amount to an impairment under the DDA.

## The impairment must be "substantial"

For an impairment to be substantial, it must be more than minor and will include an inability to take and/or remember and relay a simple message correctly or an ability to open doors or to turn taps or to press buttons.

## Long-term effects

The effects of the impairment are long-term if:

- they have lasted at least 12 months;
- the period for which they can last can reasonably be expected to be 12 months; or
- they can reasonably be expected to last for the rest of the life of the person affected.

## Recurring conditions

Long-term effects include those that are likely to recur at least once beyond the twelve-month period following the first occurrence, e.g. epilepsy.

A condition such as hay fever (where the effects may occur and be substantial for a brief time, but which could be non-existent for much of the person's life) is not regarded as "impairment" under the DDA.

## Regressive conditions

The DDA covers regressive conditions where impairments are likely to become substantial. Examples of regressive conditions include: cancer, HIV, multiple sclerosis, muscular dystrophy and motor neurone disease.

The DDA covers people with these conditions from the moment that there is a notable effect on their normal day-to-day activities, however slight.

## Genetic predispositions

The DDA does not cover people with a gene that causes their disability unless they develop the disability. Thus people with a gene that causes Huntington's Chorea are not covered if they do not have the condition.

## Past disabilities

Section 2 DDA protects "a person who has had a disability" even though he or she may no longer be disabled. The DDA, therefore, applies to those who have a history of disability as well as to those who are currently disabled. The DDA could, therefore, cover someone who has a history of heart disease and/or angina, someone who has had a serious sports injury with unforeseeable future consequences, or someone who has had a past history of mental illness.

## What are normal day-to-day activities?

Schedule 1, paragraph 4 DDA defines "normal day-to-day activities". In determining what is a normal day-to-day activity an employer should take account of how far that activity is a normal activity for most people on either a daily or fairly regular basis. The term "normal day-to-day activity" is not intended to include skilled activities which are normal only for a particular person or group of people. Thus, activities such as playing a musical instrument, or playing sport to a highly professional standard, or performing a highly skilled task at work might be regarded as "skilled activities".

Schedule 1 DDA states that an impairment is to be taken to effect the ability of the person concerned to carry out normal day-to-day activities only if it affects one of the following:

*Mobility*

Mobility covers moving or changing position in a broad sense. People who are not disabled should be able to move around unaided in order to complete their daily tasks.

*Manual dexterity*

This covers the use of hands or fingers with precision and with coordination. If an employee cannot use his or her hands or fingers to do tasks such as picking up or putting down, writing or typing, over the long term, then they are likely to be disabled.

*Physical coordination*

A lack of hand and eye coordination over the long-term may be a disability.

*Continence*

An inability to control urination and/or defecation would be a disability.

*Ability to lift, carry or otherwise move everyday objects*

A person with a disability may have difficulty or may be unable to repeat the above functions. The phrase "everyday objects" might include books, a kettle, shopping bags, a brief case, a chair or any other piece of light furniture.

*Speech, hearing or eyesight*

This category covers all day-to-day activities which involve the ability to speak, hear or see and includes face to face, telephone and written communications. Examples of the factors which an employer should consider in order to determine whether a person is disabled in these faculties include:

- Speech: employers should take into account how far a person is able to speak clearly at a normal pace and rhythm and their ability to understand someone speaking normally in his or her native language.

- Hearing: if a person uses a hearing aid and cannot hear at all or can only hear inadequately without it, then they will be covered by the DDA.

- Eyesight: a person will not be impeded from doing normal day-to-day activities if an eyesight difficulty has been corrected by spectacles or contact lenses so as to enable them to carry out their duties adequately.

- Memory or ability to concentrate, learn or understand: employers should take account of a person's ability to remember, organise his or her thoughts and their ability to plan a course of action and execute it, in deciding whether or not that person is disabled.

- Perception of the risk of physical danger: this would include an appreciation of danger in the workplace.

## Discrimination under the DDA

The DDA provides that no disabled job applicant or employee should be treated less favourably than another person, for a reason related to his or her disability unless the employer has a material and substantial reason for doing so. This means that the reason has to be related to the individual circumstances of the employer and the job applicant or employee in question and the reason must not be trivial. Thus, an assumption by an employer that disabled people are more likely to take sick leave is a stereotype and will very likely not be a material reason for not employing a disabled person. Furthermore, a belief that a disabled job applicant is likely to be slightly less efficient than a non-disabled job applicant will not be a substantial reason for refusing employment.

Under s 4 DDA employers will potentially be liable for discrimination against a disabled person in:

### *Recruitment and interviews*

> **Example**
>
> An employer requires a typist and someone with arthritis in their hands applies for the job, but their typing speed is too slow. The employer must consider whether reasonable adjustments could be

made to fit the job to the disabled person, *e.g.* by making alterations to their work station or by allowing a few more breaks than are allowed to other employees. If no reasonable adjustment can be made then the employer might be justified in not employing that person.

Employers and potential employers owe a duty to job applicants to make the premises accessible for interview and to make reasonable adjustments to accommodate interviewees.

## Promotion and transfers

### Example

An employer could not justify refusing to promote an employee with a disability, if by rearranging a work station, the disabled person could otherwise carry out the higher grade job.

## Dismissal

If a disabled employee takes time off for medical reasons, an employer would probably not be justified in dismissing the employee if the employee's absence record was not substantially worse than the employer's other employees.

## Victimisation

Section 55 DDA provides that victimisation occurs where an employer or a fellow employee ("the discriminator") treats the victim less favourably than he treats or would treat others because the victim has or the discriminator believes or suspects that the victim has or intends to:

• bring proceedings in an industrial tribunal under the DDA against the discriminator;

• give evidence in proceedings under the DDA against the discriminator;

- help someone else to bring proceedings under the DDA against the discriminator; or

- allege that the discriminator has contravened the DDA.

## Justified disability discrimination

One of the most significant differences between the DDA and the RRA and SDA, is that under the DDA, it is possible for employers to justify discrimination against disabled people.

Section 5(1) DDA provides that an employer will be treated as having discriminated against a disabled person if:

- for a reason which relates to a disabled person's disability, he treats him less favourably than he treats or would treat others to whom that reason does not or would not apply; and

- he cannot show that the treatment in question is justified.

Early drafts of the DDA identified a list of circumstances where discrimination will be justified. However it now seems that, at least for the time being, the question of justification will be left to industrial tribunals to decide on a case-by-case basis. Essentially, an employer will only be able to justify the discriminatory treatment of a disabled employee if the employer has first considered all reasonable steps to accommodate the disabled person, including making reasonable adjustments to the premises.

## The employer's duty to make reasonable adjustments

Section 6(1) DDA provides that where any arrangements made by or on behalf of an employer, or any physical features of premises occupied by the employer, place the disabled person concerned at a substantial disadvantage in comparison with persons who are not disabled, it is the duty of the employer to take such steps as it is reasonable, in all the circumstances of the case, for him to take in order for him to prevent the arrangements or feature having that effect.

The Employment Disability Regulations provide that the term "physical feature of premises" includes any of the following, whether temporary or permanent:

- any feature arising from the design or construction of a building or premises;

- any feature on the premises or of any approach to or access to a building;

- any fixtures, fittings, furnishings, furniture, equipment or materials in or on the premises;

- any other physical element or quality of any land comprised in the premises.

## Building regulations relating to disabled people

The Employment Disability Regulations provide that where buildings or extensions were constructed in accordance with building regulations relating to disabled people, then employers should not have to make a reasonable adjustment to any aspect of a feature specifically covered by those building regulations.

## Factors for an employer to consider before making reasonable adjustments

The duty to make a reasonable adjustment in s 6(1) DDA is qualified by s 6(4) which states that, in determining whether it is reasonable for an employer to take a particular step in order to comply with the duty to make reasonable adjustments, the following factors should be taken into account:

- the extent to which taking the step would prevent the effect in question;

- the extent to which it is practicable for the employer to take the step;

- the financial and other costs which would be incurred by the employer and the extent to which taking the particular step would disrupt the employer's business activities;

- the extent of the employer's financial resources;

- the availability of the financial or other assistance to the employer.

The above list is not exhaustive and may be changed by further regulations. It will be for industrial tribunals to decide in each case whether an employer acted reasonably when taking or deciding not to take any step.

## *Examples of the reasonable adjustments an employer may have to make*

Section 6(3) DDA lists the following examples of steps which an employer may have to take to comply with the duty to make reasonable adjustments:

- making adjustments to premises;

- allocating some of the disabled person's duties to someone else;

- transferring the disabled person to fill an existing vacancy;

- altering the disabled person's hours of work;

- changing the work;

- changing the place of work;

- allowing the employee to be absent during working hours for treatment, assessment or rehabilitation;

- making special arrangements for training;

- modifying equipment;

- modifying instructions or reference manuals;

- modifying procedures for tests or assessments;

- providing a reader or interpreter;

- providing supervision.

The sort of changes which employers should consider in relation to the DDA include:

- widening doorways for wheelchair access;

- changing taps to make them easier to turn;

- altering lighting for people with restricted vision;

- allocating a particular office parking space for a disabled person's car.

## What if a lease or mortgage prevents making alterations?

If an employer rents premises and the lease prevents alterations to the property, then the employer should write to the landlord or bank or building society seeking permission for the alterations.

## Others who may be made liable under the DDA

### Employers' vicarious liability for the acts of their employees

Any discriminatory act done by a person in the course of his employment shall be treated as having been done by his employer whether or not it was done with the employer's knowledge or approval (s 58(1) DDA). This means that the employer will be treated as if he had carried out the offending act himself.

### Principals and agents

A person who appoints or authorises another to be his agent with authority (which can be either expressed or implied) to act on his behalf will be liable for any discriminatory act carried out by his agent. Anything done by an agent for the principal with authority (whether that authority is expressed or implied) is treated as having been done by the principal as well as by the agent and for which both can be liable (s 58(2) DDA).

---

**Example**

A recruitment agency (the agent) appointed by an employer (the principal) could make the principal liable if with the principal's approval (whether express or implied), the agency rejected candidates with a disability because of their disability. The agent may also be liable in such circumstances.

## Principals and agents

The government proposes to make regulations to clarify the duties of principals and agents including:

- if a reasonable adjustment is necessary to enable the worker to carry out the work, without regard to the particular circumstances of the principal's business, the duty to make the adjustment will fall on the agent;

- the principal will have a duty to cooperate in the use of any equipment which is provided as an adjustment by the agent;

- where an adjustment is necessary to compensate for an effect of the principal's working arrangements or premises, the duty will fall on the principal.

## Trade unions and employers' associations

Section 13 DDA provides that it is unlawful for trade unions, employers' associations (*e.g.* the Confederation of British Industry) and professional or trade associations to discriminate against a disabled person:

- in the terms in which it is prepared to admit him to membership;

- by refusing or deliberately not accepting his application for membership.

It is also unlawful for such organisations to discriminate against a disabled person:

- in the way it affords him access to any benefits or by refusing or deliberately omitting to afford him access to them;

- by depriving him of membership, or varying the terms on which he is a member

- by subjecting him to any other detriment.

## Who can complain of disability discrimination?

In addition to potential employees and employees the following categories of worker are also protected under the DDA:

## Contract workers

A "contract worker" is a person who is employed by one individual (*e.g.* and employment agency) and who is supplied by that individual to work for another (the "principal"). A typical example of a contract worker is a temporary secretary supplied by an employment agency.

Section 12 DDA provides protection for contract workers in respect of disability discrimination. It is unlawful for a principal to discriminate against a contract worker on the grounds of disability in respect of:

- the terms on which he allows him to do contract work;
- by not allowing him to do contract work or to continue to do it;
- in the way he affords him access to any benefits, or by refusing or deliberately omitting to afford him access to them;
- by subjecting him to any other detriment.

The above protection only applies to contract work carried out at an establishment in Great Britain.

## Ill-health dismissals and disability

When dismissing an employee on the grounds of ill-health, an employer should take care to consult with the employee in order to deal with any points of conflict with the employee. Where necessary the employer should take medical advice to find out if the employee qualifies for protection as a disabled person under the DDA. The employer's medical adviser will have to consider whether the employee falls within the definition of disability in s 1 DDA.

The employer will also need to take advice on what sort of changes will have to be made to the employee's existing job or work place to accommodate the disability, and if such changes cannot be made, what kind of work the employee would be fit to do.

## Conflicting medical opinion

In many cases of dismissal on the grounds of ill-health, there is a conflict of medical opinion between the employer's doctor and the employee's own medical adviser. In such circumstances, it is open to the employer to prefer the medical advice of the employer's doctor to that of the employee's doctor. However, in doing so, the employer must act reasonably. Whether or not an employer has acted reasonably will be a question of fact to be determined by an industrial tribunal in each case.

## Enforcement, remedies, and the industrial tribunal procedure

The DDA provides that a person is entitled to complain of disability discrimination to an industrial tribunal. Where the tribunal finds the complaint is well founded, it may (if it considers that it is just and equitable):

● make a declaration;

● order the respondent to pay compensation (which compensation can be unlimited and will carry interest);

● make a recommendation.

The remedies under the DDA are the same as in the case of sex or race discrimination (see Part VI).

### The disability discrimination questionnaire

The questionnaire procedure which already applies under the RRA and SDA will be extended to complaints of disability discrimination (s 56 DDA). The procedure enables a person who considers that he or she may have been discriminated against to serve on the potential respondent a statutory form of questionnaire about the relevant facts. Whilst it is not unlawful for a potential respondent to fail to respond to the questionnaire, any such failure may lead to an inference of discrimination being drawn by an industrial tribunal.

### Settlement

Section 9 DDA makes it unlawful for an employment contract to exclude or limit the operation of the DDA. However, it will be possible to settle a claim under the DDA through ACAS (s 9 DDA) or through a statutory compromise agreement settling a complaint under the DDA (s 9(2)–(4)).

## The National Disability Council and the Northern Ireland Disability Council

The NDC and the NIDC are independent bodies set up for the purpose of advising the government on eliminating discrimination against disabled people. They will have the right to put forward measures aimed at achieving this and preparing proposals for codes of practice for employers to follow in a similar way to the CRE and the EOC in the areas of race and sex discrimination. Unlike the CRE and EOC, however, the NDC and NIDC will not have enforcement powers, nor will they be able to provide legal or financial assistance to persons who think they have been discriminated against. Contact details for the NDC and NIDC are in Appendix 4.

## Code of Practice for the Elimination of Discrimination

A draft voluntary code of practice on the employment of disabled persons has been produced by the DOE. The Code is intended to cover aspects such as:

● general guidance to help avoid discrimination;

● the main employment provisions of the DDA;

● recruitment;

● how to obtain further information and advice.

Contact details for the DOE are contained in Appendix 4.

## Summary
## Disability Discrimination

- Since 2 December 1996 the principle statute is the Disability Discrimination Act 1995 ("DDA").

- Employers with less than 20 employees at the time of the act of discrimination is committed will not be subject to the DDA.

- Under the DDA employers, are liable for discrimination against "disabled persons" in recruitment, promotion training, working conditions and dismissal.

- Unlike the RRA and SDA, the DDA provides that employers will be able to justify less favourable treatment of a disabled person by showing that the reason for such treatment is material to the circumstances of the particular case and is substantial.

- Employers are under a duty to make reasonable adjustments to the working environment where that would help overcome the practical effects of disability. What is "reasonable" will be a question of fact for an industrial tribunal to determine in each case.

- Industrial tribunals will hear complaints of disability discrimination and will be able to award unlimited compensation with interest.

- The National Disability Council and Northern Ireland Disability Council have been set up to fulfil an advisory role to the government. (See Appendix 4 for contact details.)

- A Code of Practice for the Elimination of Discrimination in the Field of Employment against Disabled Persons has been published by the DOE. (See Appendix 4 for contact details.)

# CONTENTS OF CHAPTER 4

*Age Discrimination*

# 4. AGE DISCRIMINATION

There is presently no express legislation prohibiting discrimination on grounds of age. As a general rule age limits are therefore lawful. The Labour Party has indicated that a future Labour Government would introduce legislation prohibiting discrimination on the ground of age. The Conservatives advocate a persuasive approach. An Advisory Group on Older Workers has drawn up a Code of Practice for employers on age discrimination and the Employers' Forum on Age (see Appendix 4) has been established by a group of employers to provide information and to assist employers to see the benefits of recruiting, retaining and developing older workers.

## Age discrimination and unlawful indirect sex discrimination

Age discrimination may be unlawful if an age limit amounts to indirect sex discrimination (see Chapter 2). If an age limit can be shown to be disproportionately disadvantageous to one sex then the age limit may be unlawful unless it can be shown to be justifiable.

### Examples

In the case of *Price* v *Civil Service Commission* [1978] ICR 27 the Civil Service applied an upper age limit of 28 years for applications for executive officers. Mrs Price contended that the age limit was indirectly discriminatory against women as fewer women than men could comply with it since many women in their twenties were otherwise engaged in raising a family. The EAT ruled that the age limit was discriminatory.

In *Jones* v *University of Manchester* [1993] IRLR 218 the Court of Appeal decided that a job advertisement, which stated that the University was looking to appoint graduates aged between 27 and 35, was a requirement within the SDA which discriminated against women. However, the Court of Appeal ruled that the applicant failed in her claim that the age requirement was indirectly

discriminatory on the grounds that a considerably smaller proportion of female mature students could comply with the requirement than male mature students. In other words the Applicant
failed to establish that the age limit was indirectly discriminatory
on the facts.

## Retirement ages

It is unlawful for employers to specify different retirement ages for men
and women (s 2 Sex Discrimination Act 1986). Section 126 Pensions Act
1995 provides for the equalisation of ages at which men and women can
claim the state pension and that this age should be 65. Equalisation is to
be phased in between 2010 and 2020.

Where employees have a contractual right to work beyond the normal
retirement age (NRA) – the NRA is the contractual retiring age or if there
is none or if there is no established norm, it is the age at which employees
expect to retire – employers must take care to ensure that they do not exercise their discretion disproportionately in favour of one sex or racial group.

Different treatment of men and women over the age of 60 will be
unlawful even if the motivation is to deal with inconsistencies because of
the present different state pension ages. In *James* v *Eastleigh Borough
Council* [1990] IRLR 288 the council had a policy which provided free
swimming to persons of pensionable age. This meant in practice that
women aged 60 and over and men aged 65 and over would be admitted
free of charge. Mr James who was 61, successfully complained of direct
sex discrimination. The House of Lords decided that the council's
motivation, which was not related to sex, was irrelevant to the question of
whether there had been discrimination. The test to be used was an
objective one, *i.e.* would Mr James have received the same treatment as
his wife but for his sex? The answer was yes.

In the case of *Bullock* v *Alice Ottley School* [1992] IRLR 564 the Court
of Appeal ruled that the SDA did not require a uniform retiring age for all
employees of the same employer. Mrs Bullock, a catering worker, was
dismissed when she reached 60, which was the retirement age for administrative and domestic staff as well as teachers. Gardeners and maintenance staff retired at 65. The domestic and teaching staff were in the
majority female and all the maintenance workers were male. The Court

of Appeal decided that there was neither direct nor indirect sex discrimination in this case. The court said that there was nothing to prevent an employer having a variety of retiring ages for different jobs provided that an employer's system did not involve direct or indirect discrimination based on gender.

**Summary**
**Age Discrimination**

- Age discrimination is not prohibited at present in the UK but the application of an age limit by an employer may amount to indirect sex discrimination unless it can be justified on grounds other than sex. It is unlawful to specify different retirement ages for men and women on the ground of sex.

# PART II
## Discrimination and the Offer of Work

## Introduction

Part II covers: discrimination by employers in respect of the arrangements they make for offering employment including the preparation of
job and person descriptions (Chapter 5); advertising the job (Chapter 6);
and interviewing and selecting candidates (Chapter 7). This section deals
with race, sex and disability discrimination together as, broadly, the same
rules apply to all three forms of unlawful discrimination. However, regulations are awaited concerning the offer of work and disability discrimination. As the DDA (see Chapter 3) came into force on 2 December 1996
there are, at the time of writing, no cases which can illustrate how the
DDA will be applied in practice.

# CONTENTS OF CHAPTER 5

*Job and Person Descriptions*

# 5.  JOB AND PERSON DESCRIPTIONS

## The job description

Before an advertisement is placed advertising a vacancy, an employer should prepare a job description which sets out the fundamental requirements of the job and the specific qualifications (if any) which are required to meet those requirements. The employer should bear in mind that overseas qualifications which are equivalent to UK qualifications should be considered as being as acceptable as UK qualifications to meet the requirements of the job. A good job description will neither overstate nor understate the requirements of the job, and will set out:

- the specific skills for the job;
- the qualifications required;
- the knowledge and personal qualities required to perform the job effectively and safely.

Job descriptions should be reviewed periodically, (particularly before advertising a job, see Chapter 6), to ensure that they are accurate and up to date and that they do not reflect personal or old prejudices which may disadvantage ethnic minorities, people with disabilities and members of one sex.

Great care must be taken to ensure that a job description does not contain requirements and conditions which are discriminatory. Thus, s 38(3) SDA makes clear that the use of words in a job description or advertisement with a sexual connotation such as "waiter", "sales girl", "postman" or "stewardess", shall be taken to indicate an intention to discriminate unless the job description or advertisement contains an indication to the contrary, *e.g.* by making it clear that the job is open to persons of either sex.

## "Person specifications"

One method to help both employers and interviewers, is the drawing up of a "person specification" which mirrors the job description and which describes the fundamental requirements for the person who is to perform the job. A potential employer should:

- Remember that it is the person's ability to do the job which is important. Unrelated and irrelevant personal characteristics should not
  be considered.

- Not overstate the paper qualifications that are required for the job and
  should consider the candidate's overall personality and experience and
  weigh those factors against the job description.

- Remember that the potential employer's personal feelings and
  prejudices are not factors which should be allowed to influence his
  judgment at interview.

- Consider that the candidate selected should be the one most capable of
  fulfilling the requirements of the job description.

As with a job description, a person specification should be updated regularly, particularly before advertising a post. The person specification
should be kept under review during the selection process.

**Summary**
**Job and Person Descriptions**

- Before advertising a vacancy, sending out application forms or interviewing prospective candidates, employers should prepare job and person descriptions which are objective, which set out the fundamental requirements for the job, and which form the basis upon which candidates are selected.

- Job and person descriptions should be reviewed regularly to avoid old prejudices.

# CONTENTS OF CHAPTER 6

## *Advertising the Job*

# 6. ADVERTISING THE JOB

## The law on discrimination and job advertisements

Discrimination in job advertisements is covered by s 29 RRA, s 38 SDA and s 11 DDA. Generally, it is unlawful to publish an advertisement which indicates or which might indicate, an intention to commit an act of discrimination, *e.g.* by preferring people from a particular ethnic background, or sex, or by indicating that disabled candidates will not be considered for a job. The onus is on the employer not to publish advertisements which are potentially discriminatory.

## What is a job advertisement?

An advertisement is a notice aimed either at the public generally or at a smaller group. The following are examples of advertisements:

- a notice of an internal vacancy ;
- a notice on factory gates;
- a notice on an internal notice board;
- a notice in an internal bulletin or newsletter;
- a notice appearing in a local, national or other newspaper or publication;
- a radio or television advertisement;
- a notice placed in a shop window or in a job centre;
- all notices appearing on signs, labels, show cards, goods, samples, circulars, catalogues, price lists or other material, pictures, models or films or other media.

### *How should employers prepare advertisements to avoid discrimination?*

Employers should consider the following:

- While an advertisement will try to "sell" the job it should state clearly what the objective relevant criteria for the job are, *i.e.* the skills which are required.

- An advertisement should avoid prescribing requirements such as length of residence or experience in the UK, which requirements may discriminate against job candidates from overseas.

- Where a particular qualification is required, it should be made clear that a fully comparable qualification obtained overseas is as acceptable to the employer as a UK qualification.

- Employers should ensure that an advertisement is as widely published as possible so as to reach the largest pool of potential candidates in order to avoid drawing candidates from one racial group which may dominate in a particular area to the exclusion of others.

- Employers should take care to ensure that advertisements do not appear only in areas or publications which will greatly reduce the number of applications from a particular racial group, *e.g.* by not advertising in an area with a high Afro-Caribbean population.

- If literature is sent to job applicants by the employer, it should contain a statement that the employer is an equal opportunities employer and/or contain encouraging statements such as "this business is an equal opportunities employer and we welcome applications from anyone irrespective of colour, ethnic origin, sex, marital status or disability". A reference to an equal opportunities policy in advertisements will help to project a positive image of an employer's business and may help to deflect allegations that an employer has discriminated in the selection process.

- Employers should review and update advertisements regularly to ensure that they remain appropriate.

- If an employer uses illustrations in recruitment advertisements or brochures, such illustrations should include people from ethnic minorities, women and people with disabilities. It will be particularly encouraging to show such people in positions of responsibility.

- Employers who use the "disability symbol" should ensure that it appears in advertisements.

A guiding principle for employers is to remember the description of good advertising contained in the British Code of Advertising Practice, that all advertisements should be "legal, decent, honest and truthful".

There are some exceptions to the general rule that advertisements must not discriminate. However, great care should be taken when preparing the advertisement, based on any one of the exceptions set out below. The dangers of discrimination abound and discussing the proposed advertisement with the Jobcentre first, or with your solicitor, or other employment adviser should be considered, and may help you to avoid an investigation by the CRE or EOC (see Chapter 31).

## Exceptions where discrimination is allowed in advertisements

- Jobs where being of a particular sex or race is a GOQ. (See Chapters 1 and 2.)

- Advertisements for jobs outside Great Britain can indicate the need for a person to be of a particular nationality, but cannot discriminate in terms of colour, race or ethnic or national origin.

- Positive sex, race and disability discrimination in advertisements is permitted in certain circumstances. In particular, an employer may encourage persons of a particular sex or racial group to apply for work, provided that in the last 12 months:

  –       there have been no persons of that sex or particular racial group amongst those doing that work at the employer's establishment or

  –       the proportion of persons of that sex or racial group doing the work in the employer's workforce is small when compared with the proportion of persons of that group either (a) among all those employed by the employer; or (b) among the population in the area in which the employer normally recruits persons for work in his employment.

To establish whether representation by a particular sex or racial group is small, the employer will need to ascertain the number of people of that sex or from the particular racial group in the workforce doing the particular work, and express this as a percentage of all those doing that work for the employer. The result should be compared with the percentage which that sex or racial group forms of the workforce as a whole or in the population from which the employer normally recruits for that work. Where an employer does want to encourage applicants from an under-represented group it is permissible to say in an advertisement, for example:

"Whilst selection of job candidates will be on merit alone, people of Asian origin are under-represented in this occupation and facility. Applications from such people are warmly welcomed."

The purpose of the positive discrimination exception is to help job advertisements reach members of the relevant group and to encourage their applications. It does not mean that employers should select candidates in a discriminatory way (see Chapter 7).

## Disability

The Code of Practice published by the Department of Education and Employment in connection with the DDA recommends that employers should avoid advertisements which suggest (or which might be taken to suggest) that the employer would prefer candidates who are not disabled. Otherwise the employer will need to be able to justify any adverse treatment of any disabled person who applies (see Chapter 3). Unlike under the RRA or SDA a disabled person will only be able to complain of discrimination when they have applied for the advertised post and have been rejected for it on the grounds of disability.

## Advertising through employment agencies, job centres, careers offices and schools

When recruiting through employment agencies, job centres, careers offices and schools, it is unlawful for employers to give instructions to such bodies to discriminate, *e.g.* by indicating that certain groups will or will not be preferred (ss 30 RRA, 39 SDA).

### Example

In *Hussein* v *Saints Complete House Furnishers* [1979] IRLR 337 an employer told a careers officer that he did not want to recruit from a certain area of Liverpool. Fifty per cent of the people in that area were black. The black population of Merseyside as a whole represented under 5 per cent of the total population. The

> requirement, therefore, excluded a larger proportion of black
> people than white and was indirectly discriminatory.

It is also unlawful for employers to put pressure on agencies to
discriminate against members of a particular sex or racial group (ss 31
RRA, 40 SDA).

In order to avoid indirect sex or race discrimination, (see Chapters 1
and 2), the EOC and CRE recommend that employers should not confine
advertising and recruitment unjustifiably to those agencies, job centres,
careers offices and schools which, because of their particular source of
applicants, provide only or mainly applicants of a particular racial group.

Employers should also make clear to any employment agency that they
use that the employer is an equal opportunities employer and that no
discrimination will be tolerated.

## Recruitment through employee or trade union recommendations

The EOC and CRE recommend that employers should not seek to recruit
solely, or in the first instance, through the recommendations of existing
employees, where the workforce is predominantly of one sex or racial
group, or to appoint applicants who are wholly or mainly supplied by trade
unions, where this means that only members of a particular sex or racial
group, or a disproportionately high number from that group come forward.

## Complaints and penalties in relation to a discriminatory advertisement?

Only the EOC or CRE can take proceedings for breaches of ss 29 RRA
and 38 SDA. An individual who wants to complain that an advertisement
discriminates on the grounds of race or sex must therefore ask the CRE
or EOC to act on his or her behalf. The remedy is a declaration by an
industrial tribunal that the advertisement is unlawful. If, notwithstanding
such a declaration, the CRE or EOC believes that the employer/advertiser
is likely to continue advertising in a discriminatory way, they can apply
to a county court (or in Scotland, to a Sheriffs Court) for an Order
restraining the advertiser from discriminating in the future.

As an alternative to starting proceedings before a tribunal, the CRE or EOC can carry out an informal investigation and issue a non-discrimination notice (ss 58 RRA, 67 SDA) (Chapter 31).

An individual may be able to pursue a claim personally if he or she can show that the advertisement breaches s 4(1)(1) RRA or s 6(1)(a) SDA, in that the employer is discriminating in the arrangements made for determining who is offered the job. However, in *Cardiff Women's Aid* v *Hartup* [1994] IRLR 390 the EAT decided that an advertisement did not form part of such arrangements, and therefore the individual could not pursue a claim herself.

## Disability

Under the DDA only a disabled person who has applied for a job and been rejected for it can bring a claim under the DDA. As the powers of the NDC and NIDC will not extend to prosecuting industrial tribunal proceedings for disabled people, it is likely that it will be for individuals to pursue claims against employers who discriminate in advertisements.

## Intention to discriminate

An employer will not be able to argue that he did not "intend" to discriminate in any advertisement. A court or tribunal must decide whether an advertisement is discriminatory by applying a test of what the ordinary and reasonable person would understand the advertisement to mean.

---

**Example**

Employers should avoid advertisements which illustrate an all white work force.

---

## Who is liable for discriminatory advertisements?

The employer, advertiser and publisher can all be liable for discriminatory advertisements. However, a publisher does have a defence if he proves that he published in good faith and in reliance on a statement by the employer and/or advertiser that the advertisement would not be unlawful and that it was reasonable for him to rely on that statement. Furthermore, it is a criminal offence, punishable with a fine, for an advertiser, knowingly or recklessly, to make a statement to a publisher that an advertisement is not unlawful which is false or misleading in a material respect.

**Summary**
**Advertising the Job**

- The guidelines in this Chapter apply to race, sex and disability discrimination.

- Job advertisements should be published as widely as possible and should contain a statement that the employer is an "equal opportunities employer".

- Employers are allowed (in limited circumstances) to discriminate positively in advertisements, although great care should be taken when preparing such advertisements.

- Advertisements should be legal, decent, honest and truthful.

- If advertising through employment agencies, job centres, careers offices and schools, employers should take care that instructions are not given to such bodies to discriminate, *e.g.* by indicating that certain groups will or will not be preferred for the job.

- Employers should avoid recruiting through employee or trade union recommendations in the first instance where the workforce is predominantly white or black, male or female.

- Employers, advertisers and publishers can all be liable for discriminatory advertisements

- Discriminatory advertisements can lead to industrial tribunal proceedings against both the employer by the CRE and EOC, as well as by individuals under the RRA, SDA and DDA.

# CONTENTS OF CHAPTER 7

*Application Forms, Short Lists and Interviews*

# 7. APPLICATION FORMS, SHORT LISTS AND INTERVIEWS

## Introduction

It is important that both an employer and an employer's managers who are responsible for recruitment are thoroughly prepared for the whole recruitment process. Ideally, all staff involved in recruitment should be given training to minimise the risk of discriminatory attitudes affecting decisions which could give rise to liability under the anti-discrimination legislation. Such training should cover interviewing techniques as well as some of the legal pitfalls. Throughout all stages of the recruitment process, candidates should be assessed only against the job description and person description (see Chapter 4).

## Application forms

Employers should not use application forms as a means to discriminate against job applicants.

### Example

In *Isa & Rashid* v *British Leyland Cars Ltd* COIT 1107/125 two Pakistani job applicants were required to complete the application forms in their own handwriting. Neither of them could read or write in English and they were unable to complete the forms. The requirement that they should complete their application forms in their own handwriting was discriminatory because an ability to read and write was not a requirement for the labouring jobs for which they were applying.

The CRE code makes clear that employers should not require a standard of English higher than that needed for the safe and effective performance of the job and, in particular, employers should not disqualify applicants because they are unable to complete an application form unassisted, unless personal completion of the form is a valid test of the standard of English required for the safe and effective performance of the job.

## Disability discrimination

The Code of Practice suggests that a statement that the employer welcomes applications from suitable people with disabilities would be a positive and public statement of the employer's recruitment policy.

## Short lists

Even before the first interview, an employer's personal prejudices can appear at the stage of drawing up a short list.

### Example

An employer omits from a short list a female candidate, a black candidate or a disabled candidate who is better qualified for the job than a male, white or able bodied candidate who is short-listed. Such exclusions from short lists are discriminatory because the employer has denied the candidates the opportunity to be considered for the job. If the aggrieved candidate complains to an industrial tribunal of discrimination in these circumstances, he or she is likely to succeed with the complaint.

## Interviews

It is important to remember that employers can be liable for their employees' acts of discrimination. Thus, all reception staff should be told to treat all visitors irrespective of race, sex or disability in a courteous manner. Interviewers should be courteous, interested and should ask relevant questions. Interviewers should not be hostile or superficial and should not appear obviously disinterested in the candidate.

A good interviewer will:

- have read the candidate's application form carefully;

- have considered the requirements for the job and will be ready to put these to the candidate;

- try to put the candidate at ease by being interested and considerate;

- make notes as the interview goes along and keep the notes of the interview for the purpose of comparing candidates;

- notify both the successful and unsuccessful candidates of the outcome of the interview.

Interviewers should ensure that they are consistent in their questioning of all candidates. Examples of potentially discriminatory questions that interviewers should avoid are set out below. These examples are not exhaustive.

## Race discrimination

Interviewers should avoid asking questions such as:

- Will you need to go home to visit your relatives?

- Will you be available for work on religious festivals?

- Where did you learn to speak English?

- Can you read or write?

Interviewers should also avoid asking general knowledge questions the answers which are less likely to be known by ethnic minority candidates and which are irrelevant to the job.

## Sex discrimination

Female job applicants should not be asked the following questions:

- Are you thinking of starting a family?

- How will you look after your children and arrange child care if you have to work additional hours?

- What are your child care arrangements?

- What will you do if your children are sick?

- Will your children and/or partner mind if you work long hours?

- Will you move job if your partner has to move his job?

- Will you be able to be "one of the boys"?

Male applicants should not be asked:

- Do you consider this to be woman's work?

- Your boss is a woman. Does that concern you?

- Will it hurt your pride to work for a woman?

- Will you be able to be "one of the girls"?

If a woman or man is asked questions similar to those listed above which are not also asked of candidates of the opposite sex, then he or she has been treated less favourably on the grounds of his or her sex in the arrangements for the job and the interviewer is guilty of direct sex discrimination (Chapter 2).

Furthermore, if as a consequence of asking the discriminatory questions, the candidate is not appointed, the decision not to appoint the candidate may itself be discriminatory and could give rise to an industrial tribunal claim.

## Disability discrimination

Potential employers should ask candidates in advance of an interview whether they have special requirements so that the employer can make adequate preparation for any reasonable adjustment to their premises in preparation for the interview (see Chapter 3). An employer may have to make an adjustment even if someone turns up for an interview when the employer did not know in advance that the candidate was disabled.

Interviewers should try particularly hard to put candidates with disabilities at their ease by emphasising that disability does not affect the consideration that they will receive. Interviewers should only ask about a candidate's disability if it is relevant to do so. Interviewers should concentrate upon the person's ability to do the job – after a reasonable adjustment has been made, if necessary (see Chapter 3). In asking questions about disability, interviewers should not treat a disabled person less favourably than others without justification.

The Employers' Forum on Disability (see Appendix 4) has published a leaflet entitled "Disability Etiquette" which contains guidance for employers on meeting, interviewing and working with disabled persons.

## Question and answer sheets and interview notes

It is useful for an interviewer to have a question and answer sheet at interview. Ideally, this should be completed as each question is answered by the candidate, or if this is not possible, immediately following the interview. Such a procedure can ensure that the fundamental requirements for the job are put to and discussed with the candidate. Such a format does not mean either that the interviewer should follow the sheet slavishly or should not ask questions outside of the "question and answer" sheet.

Interviewers should remember that notes of the interviews can be requested to be disclosed at industrial tribunals and written remarks on the notes such as "she was not good looking" or "not English enough" (even if written for private amusement) will be strong evidence to an industrial tribunal that the employer intended to discriminate when interviewing candidates.

**Summary**
**Application Forms, Short Lists and Interviews**

- Staff should be given training in dealing with the recruitment process to minimise the risk of discrimination.

- A higher standard of English should not be required to complete application forms than is required for the safe and proper performance of the job.

- Short lists should include all candidates who appear best qualified for the job (giving equal status to overseas qualifications which are equivalent to UK qualifications).

- Interviewers should only ask relevant questions and should not allow their personal prejudices to enter the questioning. If a candidate is asked discriminatory questions, the decision not to appoint that candidate may give rise to a claim in an industrial tribunal for discrimination.

- Interviewers should prepare question and answer sheets to follow at interviews.

- Employers should keep records of interviews to ensure that interviews are being carried out consistently.

# CONTENTS OF CHAPTER 8

*The Job Offer*

# 8. THE JOB OFFER

## Refusing or omitting to offer employment

Section 4(1) RRA, s 4(1) SDA and s 4(1)(c) DDA make it unlawful for a person to discriminate against another person by refusing or omitting to offer him employment. Employers should not, for example:

- Tell a potential applicant of a particular sex, race, or colour, or a disabled applicant, not to apply for the job.

> ### Example
>
> In a sex discrimination case, a woman was prevented from applying for a job because the employer felt that the work was "too strenuous". An industrial tribunal upheld the woman's complaint and ruled that the employer's act was direct discrimination as the woman was physically capable of doing the job. The employer had made it abundantly clear that it would not employ a woman (*Bolton* v *Nacanco Ltd* COIT 746/78

- Tell an applicant from an ethnic minority group that a job vacancy is filled when it is not. This is direct race discrimination (*Johnson* v *Timber Tailors (Midlands) Ltd* [1978] IRLR 146).

- Reject a candidate for a job from an ethnic minority when that candidate has qualifications and experience superior to those of the successful English candidate. In the absence of evidence from the employer to prove that the English candidate was better suited to the job, (*i.e.* by their performance at the interview), an industrial tribunal has found that the employer had directly discriminated against the ethnic minority candidate. (*Noone* v *Northwest Regional Health Authority* [1988] IRLR 195).

- Reject a candidate with a disability without considering first whether a disabled candidate would actually be a better person for the job than any other applicant (after any appropriate reasonable adjustment – see Chapter 3)).

## *Job descriptions etc are disclosable in industrial tribunal proceedings*

Industrial tribunals can order that all relevant documents (including job descriptions, application forms, interview notes, etc) relating to the entire candidate selection process should be produced at a hearing to investigate complaints of discrimination.

A tribunal has the power to investigate why a complainant candidate was not appointed for the job, and to compare the complainant's qualifications, experience and general suitability as against other candidates including the successful candidate. In the absence of an explanation from the employer as to why the minority candidate was not selected for the job, it is likely that the tribunal will draw an inference that the employer intended to discriminate against the minority candidate.

Employers should, for at least 6 months after the appointment of a candidate, keep records of job applications from all candidates for the job. If the employer is a large organisation with a number of persons responsible for interviewing and selecting candidates, the records from each person responsible for interviewing and recruiting should be reviewed periodically to try to avoid acts of discrimination taking place.

**Summary**
**The Job Offer**

- It is unlawful for an employer to discriminate against another person by refusing or omitting to offer employment to that person on discriminatory grounds, *e.g.* by telling a potential candidate of a particular sex or race or a candidate with a disability not to apply for a job.

- Employers should not reject ethnic minority candidates who have qualifications and experience superior to those of an indigenous applicant.

- Employers should not reject disabled candidates without first considering whether, after reasonable adjustments, a disabled candidate might be the best person for the job.

- Industrial tribunals investigating a complaint of discrimination can call for all documents generated during the recruitment process.

# CONTENTS OF CHAPTER 9

*Training*

# 9. PRE-EMPLOYMENT TRAINING, PRE-RECRUITMENT TRAINING AND POSITIVE ACTION TRAINING

## Pre-employment training

Pre-employment training helps employers to recruit unemployed people, amongst whom those from ethnic minorities and those with disabilities are often represented. The scheme, run by the DOE (see Appendix 4), enables employers to participate in training courses which unemployed people can attend while continuing to draw unemployment benefit. If employers arrange this training themselves, they must negotiate unemployment benefit arrangements with their local Unemployment Benefit Office or job centre. There are two main types of pre-employment training: pre-recruitment training and customised training.

## Pre-recruitment training

Pre-recruitment training aims to help long termed unemployed people to compete for jobs. The Employment Service arranges and finances training on behalf of employers so long as employers are prepared to guarantee job interviews for those who complete it. Employers should make sure that all courses are open to everyone regardless of race, sex, or disability. The courses are called "Job Preparation Courses" and are run under the Employment Service "Job Interview Guarantee Initiative". The courses explain what an employer is looking for in recruits; how to complete application forms and behave at interviews; and may familiarise applicants with psychometric or other recruitment tests used by the employer. The courses can include a visit to the employer's place of business and the employer is expected to participate in the course and to give information about the employer's business. Further information about pre-recruitment training can be obtained from jobcentres.

## Customised training

The employer designs a training programme to train people for specific job vacancies. Customised training concentrates on the specific skills required to do the job and provides a period of practical work experience. Jobcentres, local training enterprise councils and local enterprise companies can provide information to assist employers plan customised training programmes.

## Positive action training

Positive action training includes a range of measures which employers can lawfully take to encourage and train those from a particular racial group or sex or disabled persons, who are under represented in the employer's workforce, in order to help them overcome disadvantages in competing with other candidates. Whilst candidates selected for the job must be selected on the basis of merit alone, employers can:

- Encourage people of a particular racial group or sex or disabled persons to take advantage of opportunities to do particular work in which they are under-represented in the employer's workforce.

- Train people from a particular racial group or sex or disabled persons for particular work which the employer has and in which such persons are under represented.

- Section 35 RRA allows both employers and training bodies to restrict training to members of a particular racial group where it meets the special needs of that group. The word "special" means different training rather than greater training. For example, a course on English language specifically designed for speakers of a different language might well be covered by s 35 RRA. A GCSE English language course arguably would not be able to meet the "special needs" of a particular racial group, because many people from all racial groups would benefit from a GCSE English course.

Employers should note that, as "positive action" may involve giving special attention to a particular racial group or to one sex or to persons with a disability, it is very important that they ensure that the action they propose is within the law. Employers are strongly advised to consult their legal or other advisor on proposals for positive action training before putting them into effect. The CRE, EOC, NDC or NIDC are also be able to give advice.

### Summary
### Pre-employment Training, Pre-recruitment Training
### and Positive Action Training

- The Department of Education and Employment encourages employers to offer pre-employment, and pre-recruitment and positive action training to ethnic minority candidates and other disadvantaged persons (including those with disabilities) where such training will meet the "special needs" of the disadvantaged group.

- Employers should take care that any training given is within the law and should seek advice before introducing pre-employment training and positive action training.

# PART III
*Discrimination at Work*

## Introduction

Part III illustrates potential areas for discrimination after recruitment and during the employment relationship.

# CONTENTS OF CHAPTER 10

*Discrimination and the Terms and Conditions of Employment*

# 10. DISCRIMINATION AND THE TERMS AND CONDITIONS OF EMPLOYMENT

## Particulars to be given in the terms and conditions

Not later than 2 months after the beginning of employment, an employer is obliged to give to a new employee a written statement containing the following particulars required by s 1 ERA 1996:

- the name of the employer;
- the name of the employee;
- the date on which employment began;
- the date on which the employee's period of continuous employment began, taking into account any employment with a previous employer which counts towards that period;
- the scale or rate of remuneration or the method of calculating remuneration;
- the intervals at which remuneration is paid;
- the hours of work including any terms and conditions relating to normal working hours;
- holiday entitlement;
- terms and conditions relating to any incapacity for work due to sickness or injury, including any provision for sick pay;
- the length of notice to be given by the employer to the employee to terminate the contract of employment;
- the length of notice to be given by the employee to the employer to terminate the contract of employment;
- where the employment is not intended to be permanent, the period during which it is expected to continue or, if the employment is for a fixed term, the date on which the fixed term will expire;
- the employee's job title or a written description of the work which the employee has been recruited to carry out;

- the employee's place of work or, where the employee is required to work in various places, an indication that this is the case and details of the main address of the employer;

- any collective agreements which directly affect the terms and conditions of the employment, including, where the employer is not a party, details of the persons who are parties to any collective agreement;

- where the employee is required to work outside the UK for a period of more than one month, information about the period of work outside the UK; the currency in which payment will be made; additional pay and benefits to be provided whilst the employee is working outside the UK; and any terms and conditions relating to the employee's return to the UK;

- a note specifying any disciplinary agreements and rules which may apply to the employment.

Employers should take care to ensure that they act consistently when offering terms and conditions of employment and that they do not discriminate against employees on the grounds of race, sex or disability, unless in the case of disabled persons that discrimination is justified. (See Chapter 3). Employers should note that they can still be liable for discrimination even if the terms they offer to a candidate for a job are rejected by the candidate.

## Examples

In *O'Rourke* v *Grand Met Scottish Site Services Ltd* SCOIT S/913/77 two women were recruited as catering assistants at a site in the Shetlands, but were not offered the free accommodation and meals which male catering assistants enjoyed, nor were they compensated for the difference. They had been directly discriminated against on the ground of sex.

In *Dunlop* v *Royal Scottish Academy* SCOIT S/3696/76, a female student hired for a temporary holiday job as a security guard was told that she would not be allowed to work on night shifts as that was a job to be carried out by men. As a result she lost earnings and a tribunal held that she had been discriminated against on the ground of sex.

Employers should be particularly careful to avoid discriminating against women in the amount of pay and benefits offered to women under a proposed contract of employment. If the woman accepts an offer on lower remuneration than is offered to male workers doing the same job then she may have a claim under the Equal Pay Act 1970 (EqPA) (see Chapter 14).

## Disability discrimination

Under the DDA employers are encouraged to provide special equipment and to make reasonable adjustments to help people with disabilities. (See Chapter 3.)

**Summary**
**The Terms and Conditions of Employment**

- Not later than 2 months after the beginning of an employee's employment with an employer, the employer is obliged to give to the employee a written statement setting out certain particulars.

- Employers should act consistently when offering terms and conditions of employment and should not discriminate against employees on the grounds of race, sex or disability (unless discrimination against a disabled person is justified – see Chapter 3) in the terms and conditions offered. If men or women are discriminated against in the amount of pay and benefits offered to them then such discrimination could give rise to a claim under the EqPA (see Chapter 14).

# CONTENTS OF CHAPTER 11

## *AIDS and HIV*

# 11. AIDS AND HIV

## Introduction

AIDS and HIV have been the source of much fear and misconception in society, particularly concerning the ways in which the HIV virus can be transmitted from one person to another. As a result many workers find themselves being discriminated against, and many employers are confronted by employees who refuse to work with people who are, or whom they believe to be, carrying the HIV virus or suffering from AIDS.

It is important that employers take steps to educate their employees about HIV and AIDS and remove the many myths surrounding the risk of infection in the work place.

## Disability discrimination

Individuals who are HIV positive or who have AIDS have no specific protection under UK or EC law. However they may in some cases have claims for disability discrimination.

HIV is one of the regressive conditions covered by the DDA (see Chapter 3), and employees who are HIV positive or who have AIDS will be protected by the DDA as soon as there is a notable effect on their normal day to day activities.

## Dismissals connected with HIV and AIDS

Very few unfair dismissal claims concerning HIV and AIDS have reached industrial tribunal hearings, the problem faced by many employees with HIV/AIDS who have been dismissed due to their condition being that they did not have sufficient continuous service with their employers.

Where the employee does have sufficient continuous service and the dismissal was on the grounds that he or she has HIV/AIDS, a claim for unfair dismissal is likely to succeed.

The employer may be able to argue that the dismissal is fair for "some other substantial reason" under s 98(1) ERA if, due to the nature of the employee's work, there is a real risk that other employees or the general public may become infected. This is likely to be the case in health care and one or two other areas, but otherwise an employee with HIV/AIDS will pose no threat to his or her colleagues from ordinary work and contact. Even where a real risk of infection exists, a dismissal will only be fair if there is no suitable alternative work available for the employee which does not involve the same risks.

The employer may also be able to rely on "some other substantial reason" where genuine business difficulties are caused by other employees refusing to work with an HIV infected person. In this situation the employer would have to show that he has taken all reasonable steps to consult and inform the workers about the realities of HIV and convince them that their fears are misguided.

If an employee becomes incapable of carrying out his or her duties because of an AIDS related illness, the employer must follow the same sickness procedure which would apply to any other employee absent through illness before resorting to dismissal. This means that the employer must carry out a proper investigation, obtain medical reports, consult with the employee and consider whether there is any alternative work which the employee could do.

## HIV testing

### Testing during recruitment

Employers are entitled to request an HIV test during recruitment, although the test may only be carried out with the job applicant's consent.

In *X* v *Commission of the European Communities* [1995] IRLR 320 Mr X applied for work with the Commission as a typist. He underwent a clinical examination by the Commission's medical officer, supplemented by biological tests. However he refused to be screened for HIV antibodies. As a result of the medical examination and Mr X's medical history, the medical officer ordered blood tests to determine the T4/T8 lymphocyte count, which might point to the presence of the HIV virus. From these tests, the medical officer concluded that Mr X had "full-blown AIDS". Mr X claimed that he had been subjected to an HIV test without his consent, and that this was contrary to Article 8 of the European Convention on Human Rights. This provides that:

"Everyone has the right to respect for his private and family life, his home and his correspondence.

There should be no interference by a public authority with the exercise of this right except such as is in accordance with the law and is necessary in a democratic society in the interests of national security, public safety or the economic well being of the country, for the prevention of disorder or crime, for the protection of health or morals, or for the protection of the rights and freedoms of others."

The ECJ ruled that the right to respect for private life means that a refusal to undergo a medical test must be respected in its entirety. Therefore, when Mr X refused to undergo screening for HIV, the Commission was precluded from carrying out not only a specific HIV test but also any other test which might indicate that Mr X was HIV positive.

The ECJ made clear that its decision in *X v Commission of the European Communities* does not affect the legitimacy of medical examinations during recruitment, and that "if the Applicant, after being properly informed, withholds his consent to a test which the medical officer considers necessary to evaluate his suitability for the post", the employer "cannot be obliged to take the risk of recruiting him".

In most cases the HIV test will be carried out by the employer's doctor as part of a complete medical examination, but if it is undertaken by the job applicant's own doctor, the employer must bear in mind the Access to Medical Reports Act 1988. This provides that:

- the employer must obtain the applicant's written consent before applying for a medical report;

- the employer must inform the applicant of his/her rights under the Access to Medical Reports Act 1988;

- the employer must notify the medical practitioner if the applicant wishes to see the report.;

- the applicant has the right to see the report before it is supplied to his/her prospective employer;

- the applicant is entitled to request the medical practitioner to amend any part of the report which the applicant considers to be incorrect or misleading, or to have a statement attached setting out the applicant's views if the practitioner cannot accede to the applicant's request;

- having seen the report, the applicant may withhold consent to its being supplied to the employer.

## Testing of existing employees

The points made above in relation to the obtaining of the job applicant's consent to an HIV test also apply to the testing of existing employees, as do the provisions of the Access to Medical Reports Act 1988.

However by requesting an HIV test of an existing employee, an employer may be acting in breach of the duty of trust and confidence which is implied into every employment contract.

In *Bliss* v *South East Thames Regional Health Authority* [1987] ICR 700 the Court of Appeal decided that the Authority's insistence that a doctor undergo a psychiatric examination was a breach of the implied term of mutual trust and confidence which underpins the contract of employment. Therefore, if an employer insists that an employee undergoes an HIV test where there is no express term in the employment contract providing for HIV testing, the employer is likely to commit a fundamental breach of the implied term of trust and confidence. This would entitle the employee to resign and claim that he or she has been unfairly constructively dismissed (see Chapter 16).

In some jobs there may be an implied right to request an HIV test, particularly where, due to the nature of the employee's job, there is a real risk of infecting other employees or the public in general.

Where there is an express or implied right to request an HIV test, the employer will not necessarily be entitled to dismiss the employee if he or she refuses to undertake the test. The employer will still have to act fairly in dismissing the employee, which means that there will have to be a good reason for requiring the test and the employee must have been warned of the consequences of his or her refusal to take the test.

## Sex and race discrimination

If an employer wishes to request an HIV test, it must do so irrespective of the person's sex and race. For example, an employer might ask only single male job candidates or employees to undergo an HIV test in the belief that they are more likely to be HIV positive than any other group. The employer's insistence on testing single males will be direct sex discrimination.

Furthermore, the testing of all job applicants or employees could amount to indirect sex and race discrimination, on the basis that, statistically, more men and more Africans are HIV positive. This means that a considerably smaller proportion of men and Africans than women and non-Africans may be able to satisfy a requirement to be HIV negative. The employer may however be able to show that the requirement to be HIV negative can be justified on non-sex and non-race grounds, *e.g.* due to the nature of the particular job.

# CONTENTS OF CHAPTER 12

## *Appearance*

# 12. APPEARANCE

## Dress codes

For many businesses a requirement that employees are smartly dressed is essential. Many employers have a "dress code" which will sometimes require women always to wear skirts and men to wear jackets and ties. Such dress codes should allow for exceptions *e.g.* on the grounds of religion or disability, and the employer should be aware that the rigid enforcement of a dress code could given rise to claims for sex, race or disability discrimination.

In cases where an employee wishes to depart from an employer's dress code, then the employer should consider the employee's reasons carefully. If, following such consideration, the employer is satisfied that it is reasonable in all the circumstances of the case to enforce the dress code, then any breaches of the dress code by the employee should be dealt with under the employer's disciplinary procedure and any complaint by the employee should be pursued under the employer's grievance procedure.

## Some problem areas

### Beards

A rule banning beards will generally not be justifiable and may well be discriminatory if it is applied to Sikhs, unless such a rule can objectively be justified.

### Example

In *Panesar* v *The Nestle Co Ltd* [1980] IRLR 60 Mr Panesar, an orthodox Sikh, was refused a job interview because of his refusal to shave off his beard. An industrial tribunal decided that whilst a smaller proportion of Sikhs than non-Sikhs could comply with the "no beards" rule and that the rule indirectly discriminated against Sikhs, the rule was justifiable as it was introduced solely in the interest of hygiene..

Generally, before imposing a ban on beards, employers should investigate all the alternative possibilities such as providing covering for beards in places where there are hygiene risks.

## Earrings

Many employers will find it unacceptable for their male employees to wear earrings, taking the view that they will portray the wrong image for their business. If there are no such restrictions on female employees, this obviously gives rise to the possibility of sex discrimination. Different courts and tribunals have reached different decisions on the issue.

In *Carpenter* v *Kennings Ltd* COIT 1571/78 the dismissal of a male driver for wearing an ear stud was held to be unlawful sex discrimination.

Similarly, in *McConomy* v *Croft Inns Ltd* [1992] IRLR 561 the Northern Ireland High Court ruled that the owner of a public house discriminated against a male customer who was refused entry because he wore earrings. The court found it "difficult to see how in today's conditions it is possible to say that the circumstances are different as between men and women as regards the wearing of personal jewellery or other items of personal adornment".

However, in *Lumber* v *Hodder t/a Athlete's Foot* COIT 1834/91 an industrial tribunal decided that the owner of a sports shop did not discriminate against a male sales assistant who was dismissed for wearing an earring. The owner wanted to convey to the public a clean-cut sporting image of his business, and the tribunal upheld his right to do so. Whilst the owner would not have objected to a woman wearing earrings, he would have objected if a woman had worn inappropriate clothes or accessories.

An employer's right to insist on conventional standards of dress and appearance which differ between men and women was endorsed by the Court of Appeal in *Smith* v *Safeway plc* [1996] IRLR 456, a case concerning rules relating to hair (see below).

The *Safeway* decision suggests that employers can prohibit male employees from wearing earrings in order to convey a conventional image of their business, provided they apply their dress codes even-handedly to men and women.

## Hair

Whilst the requirement that all employees, regardless of sex, have "clean and tidy" hair will clearly not be discriminatory, some male employees may feel aggrieved if they are not allowed to have long hair when there are no such restrictions on their female colleagues.

> **Example**
>
> In *Smith* v *Safeway plc* [1996] IRLR 456 Mr Smith was dismissed because the length of his hair contravened his employer's rules for the appearance of male delicatessen staff. The Court of Appeal ruled that the employer's requirements did not amount to unlawful sex discrimination. Although female staff were allowed to have longer hair than male staff, the employer was entitled to impose a standard which was conventional and which was applied even-handedly to both men and women.

However not all employers will be able to rely on the *Safeway* decision and insist that their male employees have short hair.

> **Example**
>
> A male telesales operator who has no visual contact with customers is likely to succeed in a claim for sex discrimination if he is required to cut off his ponytail. Even if the employer wants to portray a conventional image of his business to customers, the employee's hair forms no part of that image.

## Cross-dressing

It is not sex discrimination to prohibit male employees from wearing a skirt or other women's clothing to work, even if their female colleagues are allowed to wear trousers (*Ryder-Barrett* v *Alpha Training Ltd* COIT 43377/91 (but see Chapter 26).

## Saris

The CRE Code of Practice recommends that, where employees have religious and cultural needs which conflict with existing working requirements, it is recommended that employers should consider whether it is reasonably practicable to vary or adapt requirements to enable such needs to be met. For example, employment should not be refused to women wearing saris or nose studs unless such refusal can be objectively justified (*e.g.* on grounds of hygiene).

*Statutory exception*

In *Kingston & Richmond Health Authority* v *Kaur* [1981] IRLR 337 the EAT decided that a smaller proportion of Sikhs than non-Sikhs could comply with a policy forbidding nurses to wear trousers as part of their uniform, but nevertheless decided that such a policy was justified if it was to comply with statutory rules prescribing the uniform to be worn by nurses.

## Turbans on construction sites

Section 11 Employment Act 1989 exempts Sikhs who wear turbans on construction sites from the application of any statutory provision which would otherwise require them to wear a safety helmet. If a Sikh who is not wearing a safety helmet is accidentally injured, any damages recoverable by the injured Sikh would be restricted to damages for injury that would have occurred even if he had worn the safety helmet. This concession only applies to Sikhs and only applies on construction sites.

If an employer imposes a condition that a Sikh should wear a safety helmet on a construction site, then this will be deemed to be indirect race discrimination unless he has reasonable grounds to believe that the Sikh would not wear a turban at all times on a construction site.

## Trousers

It can be discriminatory to refuse to allow Muslim women to wear trousers for genuine religious reasons.

In *Malik* v *British Home Stores* COIT 1980 a tribunal decided that a requirement that shop assistants should wear a uniform consisting of a skirt and overall, which discriminated against Muslim women, could not be justified if the commercial needs of the business were outweighed by the discriminatory effect. Evidence was produced to the tribunal that the proportion of Pakistani Muslims in Blackburn, where Mrs Malik worked, was 14 per cent, and BHS were thus discriminating against a group who might represent 14 per cent of their customers. The tribunal also believed that it would be a comparatively simple matter for BHS to modify their uniform regulations to permit Mrs Malik to wear a pair of trousers beneath her overalls.

Prohibiting female employees from wearing trousers may be sex discrimination if their male colleagues are not subject to any rules relating to their clothing and appearance. (*Stoke on Trent Community Transport* v *Cresswell* (unreported –EAT 359/93)).

However, if the male employees are, for example, required to wear a jacket and tie, there will be no discrimination. This is because the employer's clothing rules should be considered as whole, rather than garment by garment, to determine whether one sex is treated less favourably than the other (*Schmidt* v *Austicks Bookshops Ltd* [1978] ICR 85).

## Uniforms

Where both male and female employees are required to wear uniforms, the employer does not discriminate against one particular sex if the uniforms for men and women differ.

In *Burret* v *West Birmingham Health Authority* [1994] IRLR 7 a female nurse was required to wear a starched linen cap, which she found demeaning. The cap served no practical purpose, and male nurses were not required to wear them. The nurse was disciplined for refusing to wear the cap, but the EAT ruled that there was no sex discrimination. It noted that the requirement to wear a uniform applied to both men and women, and although the uniforms differed, male nurses who refused to wear their uniform would also have been disciplined.

# CONTENTS OF CHAPTER 13

*Benefits*

# 13.  BENEFITS

It is unlawful for employers to discriminate on grounds of sex, race or disability in providing benefits, facilities and services for employees (ss 4(2) RRA, 6(2) SDA, 4(2) DDA). The criteria governing eligibility for benefits, facilities or services should be examined by an employer to ensure that they are not unlawfully discriminatory.

## Meaning of benefits, facilities and services

Benefits, facilities and services provided to employees include:

- accommodation;
- bonuses;
- car expenses;
- child care facilities;
- clothing allowance;
- computers;
- holiday entitlements;
- holiday pay;
- job mobility;
- mobile telephones;
- mortgage subsidies;
- pay;
- overtime and overtime payments;
- private health cover;
- season tickets;
- sports clubs;
- subscriptions.

The above list is by no means exhaustive. Indeed, the variety of possible benefits is potentially infinite.

## Equal pay and money payments

The SDA does not apply to contractual benefits which consist of money payments (s 6(6) SDA). Complaints relating to such benefits must be pursued under the EqPa (see Chapter 14). However, the SDA does cover money payments which are not made as part of the contract of employment, *e.g.* an ex gratia bonus.

## Failure to investigate complaints

A failure to investigate or adequately pursue an employee's grievance on the grounds of race, sex or disability can amount to a refusal of access to benefits and can, therefore, be discriminatory.

## Segregated benefits

Section 1(2) RRA provides that it is unlawful for employers to provide equal, but segregated, facilities for members of different racial groups.

## Privacy and decency

It is not discriminatory to provide separate facilities for men and women on grounds of decency or privacy (see Chapter 2).

## Maternity benefits

Special benefits given to women in connection with pregnancy or child-birth *e.g.* maternity leave (see Chapter 21) do not amount to discrimination against men (s 2(2) SDA).

# CONTENTS OF CHAPTER 14

*Equal Pay*

# 14.  EQUAL PAY

The right of men and women to receive equal pay for equal work comes from two sources, European Community Law and the Equal Pay Act 1970 (EqPA) (as amended).

## The relationship between European Community law and the Equal Pay Act 1970

When the UK joined the European Union (then called the European Community) in 1973, the UK Government accepted the terms of the Treaty of Rome 1957 ("the Treaty"). Article 119 of the Treaty requires European Union Member States to "ensure and subsequently maintain the application of the principle that men and women should receive equal pay for equal work".

Under Article 119 "pay" means the ordinary, basic, or minimum wage or salary, and any other consideration whether in cash or in kind, which the worker receives directly or indirectly from the employer.

Prior to the ECJ's decision in *Barber* v *Guardian Royal Exchange Assurance Group* [1990] IRLR 240 the concept of "pay" had been considered by the ECJ in a number of cases as a result of which it was established that "pay" under Article 119 constituted:

- non-contractual benefits (*e.g.* travel facilities granted to employees after retirement);

- contractual or statutory redundancy payments;

- statutory sick pay.

Then came *Barber*, in which the ECJ decided that the above-mentioned definition of pay was wide enough to cover any benefit which a worker is entitled to receive from the employer.

The ECJ have also decided that payments under a statutory social security scheme are excluded from a claim under Article 119 as they could not be regarded as "pay" which the worker receives from the employer. It is uncertain whether statutory sick pay and statutory maternity pay paid by British employers would be regarded as Social Security benefits or as pay within Article 119.

EqPA, which came into force on 29 December 1975 is the UK government's attempt to enshrine into UK law the concept of "equal pay for equal work" envisaged by Article 119. The UK government has treated EqPA as fulfilling the UK's obligations under Article 119 and under the Equal Pay Directive 75/117 (which clarifies, rather than expands, the principle of equal pay in Article 119). As a result, EqPA is interpreted by industrial tribunals and courts in a way which accords with Article 119 and the Directive. EqPA has been amended on a number of occasions with the main objective of bringing its provisions into line with European Community law. Article 119 takes precedence over anything in EqPA which is inconsistent with it, however an applicant's claim for equal pay in the industrial tribunal or court must always be based on EqPA in the first instance. Only if EqPA fails to provide the applicant with an adequate remedy can the applicant then resort to a claim under Article 119. Usually applicants include a claim under Article 119 in any application to an industrial tribunal under EqPA so that the tribunal can consider a claim under Article 119 if the applicant's claim under EqPA does not succeed.

## The Equal Pay Act applies to men and women

EqPA applies equally to men and women. However, EqPA assumes that most applicants are women and for that reason we have adopted the same approach in the remainder of this Chapter.

## The relationship between the Equal Pay Act and the Sex Discrimination Act

As explained in Chapter 2, the SDA provides that men and women should not be discriminated against on the grounds of sex or marriage in relation to matters such as recruitment, job offers, trade union membership, training, transfer, promotion and dismissal. Such matters do not relate to "pay" and therefore any claims in relation to these matters should be brought in an industrial tribunal under the SDA. The scope of EqPA is, therefore, more limited than the SDA.

## Which workers are covered by the Equal Pay Act?

EqPA covers everyone who "is employed at an establishment in Great Britain". For the purposes of EqPA, "employed" means "employed under a contract of service or of apprenticeship or a contract personally to execute any work or labour" (s 1(1)(b) EqPA).

EqPA also covers the self-employed who provide their services to another as well as temporary and homeworkers. In *Quinnen* v *Hovells* [1984] IRLR 227 the EAT ruled that the definition of "employed" in s 1(6)(a) EqPA is a "wide and flexible concept".

## Which workers are not covered by the Equal Pay Act?

Employees who are employed outside Great Britain and members of the armed forces are excluded from the protection of EqPA (s 1(9) EqPA). EqPA does, however, apply to all other public employees except for those holding a statutory office, *e.g.* government ministers and Justices of the Peace.

## How does the Equal Pay Act achieve equal pay for men and women?

### The "equality clause"

Section 1 EqPA provides that if the terms of a contract of employment under which a woman is employed do not include (either expressly or by reference to a collective agreement) an "equality clause" then by virtue of EqPA, the contract shall be deemed to include one.

A woman is entitled to ask an industrial tribunal to compare each separate term in her employment contract with the corresponding term in her male comparator's contract (see below). If, following the complaint, a tribunal is satisfied that any term in the woman's contract is not comparable to that in her chosen male comparator's contract and that the woman's work is *like work* or is *work of equal value* or has been given a rating equivalent to that of her male comparator under a *job evaluation study* (JES) then the tribunal will operate the equality clause and will order that the woman's contract should be amended so that it is the same as that of her male comparator (*Heywood* v *Cammell Laird Ship Builders Ltd* [1988] IRLR 257).

The *Heywood* case made clear that a woman cannot run together all of the provisions in her contract relating to pay and benefits and then argue that her contract, when taken as a whole, is less favourable that the contract of her male comparator when taken as a whole. The equality clause will only be applied to each individual term of the woman's employment contract to the extent that each term is less favourable than the corresponding term in her male comparator's contract. A woman cannot rely on EqPA to argue that she ought to be paid more than a man.

## Claims under the Equal Pay Act

Equal pay claims are usually complex and will often involve a great deal of evidence gathering for the purpose of providing expert evidence to a tribunal. It is not unusual for claims under EqPA to take several years to reach a conclusion. Claims under EqPA can involve all parties concerned in a great deal of expense in both money and (for the employer) management time. Any employer facing a claim under EqPA is well advised to seek expert legal advice at an early stage.

### Time limits

Unlike in cases of unfair dismissal, there is no two-year minimum period of employment required before a claim can be brought before an industrial tribunal under EqPA. However, a claim under EqPA must be brought at any time before the end of a period of 6 months starting from the date on which the woman leaves her job.

### The comparator

The first step for a woman wishing to bring a claim under EqPA is to identify her male comparator. The comparator must be in the same employment as the woman. The comparator must be an actual and not a hypothetical man and he must be employed at the same time as the woman. This last principle has recently been doubted by the EAT in *Diocese of Hallarn Trustee* v *Connaughton* (EAT 1128/95). In the *Connaughton* case the EAT concluded that a woman could use an "immediate successor as a notional comparator".

It is for the woman to select her comparator and she may select more than one comparator. An industrial tribunal cannot substitute its own choice of comparator for the comparator selected by the woman. (*Ainsworth* v *Glass Tubes & Components Ltd* [1977] IRLR 74).

## "Same employment"

A comparator will be in the same employment as a woman if the comparator is employed by the same employer or by an associated employer at the same establishment as the woman; or at establishments which include the establishment at which the woman is employed and at which common terms and conditions of employment are observed either generally or for the relevant classes of employees.

In deciding whether employees are employed at establishments where common terms and conditions are observed, the House of Lords has recently decided in *British Coal Corporation* v *Smith* (The Times 23 May 1996) that a "broad comparison" test should be applied. In the *British Coal* case the House of Lords ruled that female canteen workers who were employed at 47 different locations could compare themselves with male comparators at 14 locations, because the terms and conditions of the female canteen workers and their male comparators were dealt with centrally by British Coal.

## Associated employers

Section 1(6)(c) EqPA provides that two employers are to be treated as associated employers if one employer is a company which is controlled either directly or indirectly by the other employer (which need not be a company) or if both are companies of which a third person has control either directly or indirectly.

If the woman and her male comparator are employed by the same employer at different establishments, then the woman must first establish that her terms and conditions are common to the terms and conditions of her male comparator.

Once a male comparator has been selected the woman must then show that she and her comparator are employed on either (i) like work, or (ii) on work rated as equivalent or (iii) on work of equal value.

## Like work

Section 1(4) EqPA defines "like work" as follows:

"A woman is to be regarded as employed on like work with men if, but only if, her work and theirs is of the same or a broadly similar nature, and the differences (if any) between the things she does and the things they do are not of practical importance in relation to terms and conditions of employment; and accordingly in comparing her work with theirs regard shall be had to the frequency or otherwise with which any such differences occur in practise as well as to the nature and extent of the differences."

There are two parts to the above definition:

- Is the woman's work the same or of a broadly similar nature to that of her male comparator?

- The differences (if any) between the woman's work and that of her comparator must not be of "practical importance" in relation to the terms and conditions of employment.

Tribunals must consider each of these parts in stages.

*Stage one*

First, in deciding whether the work of a woman and her comparator is the same or broadly similar, a tribunal should not undertake too detailed an examination. A tribunal should give general consideration to the work done by the woman and her male comparator and the knowledge and skill required to do the work. In comparing the work of the woman and that of her comparator, a tribunal must look at what each of them does in practice and should ignore any differences in the job title or job description of the woman and her comparator, if the practical tasks which they perform are the same in practice.

At Stage One, the tribunal is concerned only with the nature of the work done by the woman and her comparator and not, for example, with the qualifications of the individuals concerned or with their length of service.

### Example

In *Capper Pass Ltd* v *Lawton* [1976] IRLR 366 the EAT ruled that the work of a female cook who prepared lunches for the directors was broadly similar to the work of a male assistant chef who prepared meals for the employees in the factory.

*Stage two*

Once the tribunal has established in general terms that the work done by the woman and her male comparator is of a broadly similar nature, then the tribunal must go on to Stage Two and consider the details of the woman's job against those of her comparator. The tribunal should enquire whether the differences between the jobs are of practical importance in relation to the terms and conditions of employment.

## What constitutes a difference of practical importance?

There are no hard and fast rules about what constitutes a difference of practical importance between two jobs. Each case will be decided on its facts. Industrial tribunals should disregard trivial differences.

> ### Example
>
> A woman was employed by an employment agency to supply clients with temporary staff. Her male comparator was employed at the same agency but supplied clients with permanent staff. The industrial tribunal did not consider this a difference of practical importance between the woman's work and her comparator's work and so the tribunal awarded the woman equal pay.

*Further examples of differences of practical importance*

- Responsibility: If a man exercises greater responsibility in his job than the woman claimant, that may be a difference of practical importance justifying a pay differential, *e.g.* where the man is responsible for supervising staff and the woman is not.

- Time when work is carried out: In some cases, the time when work is carried out is irrelevant. However, in *Thomas* v *National Coal Board* [1987] IRLR 451 the EAT ruled that the additional responsibility entailed in working permanently at night, alone and without supervision, could amount to a difference of practical importance. However, if the woman and her male comparator do the same work, the mere fact that they do it at different times is of no importance. The disadvantage of working at night, or at other inconvenient times, can be compensated by an additional night shift premium or other appropriate arrangement, but there is no reason why the male comparator should receive a sum which is greater than necessary to recognise the fact that he works at night, or at other inconvenient times; and if he does, there is no reason why the woman should not be remunerated to the extent of the excess. An industrial tribunal is entitled to adjust the woman's remuneration so that it is at the same rate as her comparator's, discounting the fact that he works at inconvenient hours, and she does not (*National Coal Board v Sherwin* [1978] IRLR 122).

## Work rated as equivalent

A woman need not necessarily establish that she is employed on "like work" in order to invoke the "equality clause". The "equality clause" is similarly applicable if a woman can show that she is employed on work which has been rated as equivalent to that of her male comparator under a JES (s 1(2)(b) EqPA).

Section 1(5) EqPA states that:

"A woman is to be regarded as employed on work rated as equivalent with men if, but only if, her job and their job have been given an equal value, in terms of the demand made on a worker under various headings (for instance effort, skill, decision), on a study undertaken with a view to evaluating in those terms jobs to be done by all or any of the employees in an undertaking or group of undertakings, or would have been given an equal value but for the evaluation being made on a system setting different values for men and women on the same demand under any heading".

### What is job evaluation?

Job evaluation is a method of assessing the relative values of different jobs within an organisation. Only the job and not the person doing it is evaluated. The five main methods of job evaluation are:

- points assessment;
- factor comparison;
- job ranking;

- paired comparison;

- job classification

A valid JES must be analytical in the sense of evaluating each individual element of the job be it skill, effort, decision making etc. It is not sufficient simply to compare one job as a whole against another job as a whole.

A JES must be objective and must not itself be based on discriminatory factors, *e.g.* if a woman's job would have been given equal value to that of a man under a JES, but for the fact that the evaluation was made on a system which set different values for men and women, then an industrial tribunal would be required to adjust the results of the JES to compensate for the different evaluations.

If a woman believes that her job should be given the same rating as a man's job under a JES which has been undertaken by the employer, then the woman will be able to bring a claim for equal pay to an industrial tribunal.

Employers are not required by EqPA to undertake job evaluation. However, where a JES has been carried out, a woman will be entitled to rely upon it even if it has not been implemented by the employer. (*O'Brien and Others* v *Sim-Chem Ltd* [1980] IRLR 373).

## Work of equal value

Before 1984, EqPA provided for equal pay only where employees were employed on "like work" or where they were employed in "work rated as equivalent" under a JES. An employer could not be required to undertake a JES which meant that women who were engaged on work which was of equal value to the work of men where there was no JES had no right to claim equal pay.

From 1 January 1984, EqPA was amended by the Equal Pay (Amendment) Regulations 1983 (hereafter referred to as the 1983 Regulations), which give women and men the right to claim equal pay for work of equal value under s 1(2)(c) EqPA. The 1983 Regulations were introduced after the European Court of Justice found that the UK had failed to fulfil its obligations under Articles 119 and the Equal Pay Directive.

### Scope of equal value

Under s 1(2)(c) EqPA a right to equal pay will arise where a woman establishes that her work makes demands in terms of, *e.g.* effort required, skills required, decision making responsibilities, which are equivalent to those made upon her male comparator.

### An employer or an employee may refer a dispute to a tribunal

Section 2 EqPA provides that where a dispute arises between an employer and an employee as to whether or not the work of the woman and her comparator are of equal value then either the employer or the employee may apply to an industrial tribunal for an order declaring the rights of the employer and the employee in relation to the matter in question.

### Independent experts

Unless a tribunal is satisfied that there are no reasonable grounds for determining that the work of the woman and her male comparator are of equal value, then the tribunal must require a member of a panel of independent experts to prepare a report on whether the work of the woman and her comparator are of equal value (s 2(a), (b) EqPA).

An industrial tribunal will decline to appoint an independent expert, and the woman's equal value claim will fail, where her work and that of her male comparator have already been given different values under a valid non-discriminatory JES (see above). This is because s 2(a)(ii) EqPA requires an industrial tribunal to conclude that there are no reasonable grounds for finding that the work of a woman is of equal value to that of her male comparator if:

- their work has been given different values under a JES which complies with the requirements of s 1(5) EqPA; and

- there are no reasonable grounds to determine that the evaluation contained in the JES was made on a system which discriminates on grounds of sex.

The onus of showing that a JES satisfies the requirements of s 2(a)(ii) EqPA is on the employer (*Bromley v H & J Quick Ltd* [1988] IRLR 249).

Where an expert is appointed by an industrial tribunal, the expert will usually interview the woman, her comparator and the employer in order to collect evidence about the woman's job and that of her male comparator. The expert will then send a summary of the information he has gathered to the employer and to the woman for comment. Once the expert has received any comments, the expert is required to incorporate those comments in a report of the investigation into the jobs which is then sent to the industrial tribunal. The report must contain the conclusion of the expert as to whether the jobs are of equal value. If either the employer or the woman wish to challenge the independent expert's report, it is open to them to have their own independent expert prepare a report and give evidence at the tribunal.

## Which jobs have been found to be of equal value?

Industrial tribunals have found a number of jobs to be of equal value. Thus, in *Wells* v *F Smales & Son Ltd* COIT 1643/113 women fish packers succeeded with their claim for equal pay with a general labourer. In another case, sewing machinists in a furniture manufacturing company successfully compared their work to that of male upholsterers. However, it is important to remember that industrial tribunals will determine each case on its own facts and a decision in one case, whether favourable or unfavourable, will not automatically determine the outcome in other cases where similar jobs are being compared.

## Work of greater value

The right to claim equal pay for work of equal value covers situations where women are paid less for work of greater value than their male comparator. However, in these situations women can only claim parity of pay with their male comparator and cannot claim more pay even though their work is demonstrably of greater value than that of their comparator.

# The employer's defences under EqPA

## The material factor defence

Section 1(3) EqPA provides that an equality clause shall not operate in relation to a variation between a woman's contract and a man's contract if the employer proves that the variation is genuinely due to a material factor which is not the difference of sex and that factor:

- in the case of an equality clause falling within section 1(2)(a) (like work) or 1(2)(b) (work rated as equivalent) above, *must* be a material difference between the woman's case and the man's;

- in the case of an equality clause falling within section 1(2)(c) (work of equal value) above, *may* be such a material difference.

Where a woman establishes that her work is like work or is work rated as equivalent to that of her male comparator, an employer who then seeks to justify the differential treatment of the woman and her comparator must show that there is a material difference between the cases of the woman and her comparator and that the difference in pay is not due to some hidden element of sex discrimination.

The burden is on the employer to show that there is a genuine material difference and in order to succeed with this defence, the employer needs to establish three separate matters:

- that there is a genuine reason for the difference in pay between a woman and her male comparator;

- that the reason is material (*i.e.* "significant and relevant" – *Rainey* v *Greater Glasgow Health Board* [1987] IRLR 26);

- that the reason relied upon by the employer is not one of the difference in sex *i.e.* the reason is not tainted by sex discrimination. Thus, an employer cannot succeed with this defence by arguing that a male comparator is paid more because he is a man.

A material factor will be a factor or difference in the job between a woman and her male comparator put forward by the employer to explain the employer's reasons for the difference in treatment between the woman and her male comparator. The factors which can be advanced by an employer in justifying a difference in pay are numerous. Some examples are given below.

*Market forces*

In *Enderby* v *Frenchay Health Authority* [1993] IRLR 591 the ECJ ruled that where the state of the employment market leads an employer to increase the pay of a particular job in order to attract candidates, then such action may constitute an objectively justified economic ground for a difference in pay between the woman and her male comparator. If an industrial tribunal can determine precisely what proportion of the difference in pay is attributable to market forces, then it must accept that the pay differential is objectively justified to the extent of that proportion.

In *Rainey* v *Greater Glasgow Health Board* [1987] IRLR 26 a difference in pay between a female prosthetist and her male comparator, employed on like work but recruited from the private sector, on his existing terms and conditions when the prosthetic services was established prior to the woman's employment, was "genuinely due to a material difference (other than a difference of sex)", because the new service could not have been established within a reasonable time if the employees of private contractors had not been offered a scale of remuneration which was comparable to the remuneration that they would have received had they remained in the private sector.

*Differences in geographical location*

In *Navy, Army and Air Force Institutes* v *Varley* [1976] IRLR 408 a difference in weekly hours of work between employees on like work in London and in Nottingham was based on a long-standing geographical distinction which was capable of being a genuine material difference within s 1(3) EqPA.

*Protected pay*

Pay protection or "red circling" is a practice which often occurs when a worker or group of workers are moved to new positions where they would usually be paid less than they received in their existing posts. To encourage the workers to accept the transfer their pay is "red circled" (*i.e.* preserved at its existing level). An employer may be able to show that red circling constitutes a material factor difference to justify a pay difference within s 1(3) EqPA (*Snoxell* v *Vauxhall Motors Ltd* [1977] IRLR 123).

*Full- or part-time work*

As long as the aim of differential pay rates between part-time and full-time workers is not to exploit female labour, a distinction based on full-time or part-time work may be a material difference (*Bilka-Kaufhaus GmBH* v *Weber Von Hartz* [1986] IRLR 317).

In *Leverton* v *Clwyd County Council* [1989] IRLR 23 a woman worked 32.5 hours per week compared with her male comparator who worked 37 hours per week. She had 70 days' annual holiday compared with her male comparator's 20 days' holiday. The House of Lords decided that these were genuine material factors justifying a pay differential between the woman and her male comparator.

*Experience, qualifications and skill*

Subject to these criteria being relevant to the job in question, they are the most straightforward and obvious "material difference" justifications for pay differentials.

*Length of service*

Length of service was ruled to be a legitimate material factor in *Factor and Shields* v *E Coomes (Holdings) Ltd* [1978] ICR 1159.

*Collective bargaining*

Three separate decisions of the EAT support the idea that separate collective bargaining structures are capable of constituting a material factor defence for the purposes of s 1(3) EqPA. However, the defence will not succeed if the collective bargaining processes in question were tainted by discrimination. In *Enderby* (above) the court ruled that an employer could not rely on separate collective bargaining structures for a woman and her male comparator as a defence to justify an overall difference in pay between men and women. Thus, if women can show that they are paid less then men, it will not be enough for an employer to establish that the pay difference was arrived at after two separate bargaining processes which were not discriminatory in themselves.

*Permissible discrimination*

Section 6(1) EqPA provides that the equality clause shall not operate in relation to terms which comply with laws regulating the employment of women. (This is now of limited practical significance as many of the statutory provisions which protected women have been repealed.)

## Maternity benefits and equal pay

It is possible for an employer to provide maternity benefits to female employees without providing similar benefits to male employees.

## Remedies under the Equal Pay Act

An industrial tribunal has the power to make an order declaring the rights of the parties in relation to the matter in question or to award arrears of remuneration or damages. Payment by way of arrears of remuneration or damages is limited and cannot be awarded in respect of a time earlier than 2 years preceding the date on which the claim was started (s 2(5) EqPA).

**Summary**
**Equal Pay**

- The right of men and women to receive equal pay for equal work is derived from:

    –      the Equal Pay Act 1970 (EqPA) (as amended)

    –      Article 119 of the Treaty of Rome 1957

    –      the Equal Pay Directive 75/117 of 1975.

- Whilst EqPA applies equally to men and to women, most claimants are women.

- A claimant under EqPA can ask a tribunal to compare each term in her contract with her chosen male comparator's contract.

- If the tribunal is satisfied that a term in a woman's contract is less favourable than that in her male comparator's contract, then the tribunal will imply an "equality clause" and will order that the terms of the woman and her comparator are equalised.

- Employers can justify differences in pay if the differences are "genuinely due to a material factor which is not the difference of sex".

- Claims for equal pay are generally made to an industrial tribunal, although they can be pursued in the county court or High Court.

- Claimants must bring a claim within 6 months of leaving their employment.

- Tribunals can award damages back-dated for 2 years preceding the date on which the claim was started.

# CONTENTS OF
# CHAPTER 15

*Appraisals, Grading, Promotion and
Transfers to Other Work*

# 15.  APPRAISALS, GRADING, PROMOTION AND TRANSFERS TO OTHER WORK

## Appraisals

Many organisations now appraise staff using an appraisal form tailored to the needs of the particular organisation. Such appraisals should be based only on the requirement of the job and on the performance of the individual in relation to those requirements. When undertaking any appraisal it is advisable for management to revisit the job description and the person description (see Chapter 5).

Ideally, two managers should conduct the appraisal to help remove bias. Following any assessment the employee should have an opportunity to read the appraisal form and should be asked to sign it to confirm their agreement that it reflects accurately the appraisal interview.

If an employee claims to have been unfavourably appraised on the grounds of race, sex or disability and, if such a complaint is upheld, then the appraisal or assessment may have been conducted unlawfully because a biased appraisal may restrict the employee's opportunities for promotion in the future. (s 4(2)(b) RRA, s 6(4)(b) SDA, s 4(2)(b) DDA).

### Example

In *Bhattacharya* v *London Borough of Newham* COIT 1469/200 Mr Bhattacharya, who was Indian, was not promoted to the post of Building Controller. Instead the post was offered to a white candidate with fewer qualifications and less experience. In the absence of any convincing explanations from the employer, the industrial tribunal drew an inference of unlawful race discrimination.

Employers should ensure that opportunities for improved grading and/or promotions are offered equally to all employees. In particular, employers should ensure that training opportunities which may assist promotion are available equally to all employees.

## Transfers to other duties

Employers should be cautious when transferring employees to other
duties.

---

**Example**

In *Deson* v *British Leyland Cars* COIT 6281 Mr Deson had been
working successfully for 3 years as one of a two-man team when
a National Front member took the place of the other worker. Mr
Deson claimed that he was harassed by the newcomer and subjected to verbal abuse. As a result of these complaints, Mr Deson was
transferred to less congenial work, although there was no change in
the rate of pay he received or in his status. The tribunal ruled that
a transfer to a less attractive and less interesting job that nobody
else wanted is potentially discriminatory under s 4(2)(b) RRA.

---

## Disability

Section 4(2)(b) DDA mirrors s 4(2)(b) RRA. Regulations will be published later this year which will deal with training and career development
issues for disabled staff.

# CONTENTS OF CHAPTER 16

*Harassment*

# 16.  HARASSMENT

## What is harassment?

Harassment is not defined in the SDA, RRA or DDA, although, if it occurs, it may amount to direct sex, race or disability discrimination (see below under "Harassment as Discrimination")

## Definition of sexual harassment

In defining "harassment" the best starting point is probably the European Commission's Recommendation on the Protection of the Dignity of Women and Men at Work, and the Code of Practice on measures to combat sexual harassment, both of which were adopted by the European Commission in November 1991.

The Code defines sexual harassment as "unwanted conduct of a sexual nature, or other conduct based on sex affecting the dignity of women and men at work". This can include unwelcome physical, verbal and non-verbal conduct.

Article 1 of the Recommendation states that such conduct will be unacceptable where:

- it is unwanted, unreasonable and offensive to the recipient; and/or

- it is used as a basis for a decision which affects the recipient's employment; and/or

- such conduct creates an intimidating, hostile or humiliating work environment for the recipient.

The provisions of the Code of Practice are not legally binding, but courts and tribunals may take them into account in interpreting the SDA (*Wadman* v *Carpenter Farrer Partnership* [1993] IRLR 373).

Examples of conduct which may amount to sexual harassment include:

- making suggestive comments or gestures;

- requesting sexual intercourse or other sexual acts;

- unwanted sexual contact (*e.g.* a man brushing against a woman in a sexual way or forcing her to brush against him in order to pass him);

- making blatantly sexual remarks about another person's body (*e.g.* remarks about the size of a woman's breasts);

- leering at another person;

- displaying nude pin-ups (see below);

- indecent assault.

In *Rosse* v *Paramount House Group Ltd* (unreported – EAT 350/92), the EAT thought that an employer's instruction to an employee that she attend a meeting, at which he knew that she would be subjected to offensive behaviour, could itself amount to an act of sexual harassment.

The courts now recognise that individuals have the right to decide for themselves what causes them offence and what they regard as unacceptable behaviour (*Wileman* v *Minilec Engineering Ltd* [1988] IRLR 144).

## Definition of racial harassment

In May 1995 the CRE published a guidance booklet entitled "Racial Harassment at Work: What Employers can do about it". The booklet adopts a working definition of racial harassment as "unwanted conduct of a racial nature, or other conduct based on race affecting the dignity of women and men at work".

The CRE booklet notes that such harassment may be deliberate and conscious, but it can also be unintentional. Therefore racist banter or jibes, which the perpetrator may think amounts only to a joke, will often amount to racial harassment.

## Single acts of harassment

The victim does not have to suffer a series of acts of harassment in order to have a claim. A single act can constitute harassment, provided it is sufficiently serious.

> ### Examples
>
> In *Insitu Cleaning Co Ltd* v *Heads* [1995] IRLR 4 the EAT held
> that a manager who greeted an employee at a meeting with the
> remark "Hiya, big tits" committed an act of sexual harassment. It
> was no defence for the employer to say that, because the act had not
> been done before, the treatment could not be "unwanted".
>
> Similarly, in *Seventi* v *Britvic Soft Drinks Ltd* COIT 3026/8 a man's
> remark to a woman in front of her colleagues that she should
> "get her tits out" was sexual harassment. Although it was a single
> act the tribunal ruled that it was sufficiently serious to amount
> to discrimination.

## Victims who do not complain

The perpetrator of the harassment may try to claim that he was unaware
that his acts were "unwanted" because the victim had not previously
objected to his conduct. Just because the victim has not complained does
not mean that the treatment is wanted. The victim may find it difficult to
object due to the status of the perpetrator, the fear of being dismissed or
because the employer is unlikely to treat the matter seriously.

## Acts not aimed at the victim

An act may amount to harassment even if it is not aimed at the victim.

> ### Example
>
> In *Ampadu* v *Mullane* (unreported – COIT 2947/201), the landlord
> of a pub played a video of a Jim Davidson "live" act in the bar at
> the request of some customers who were having a birthday party.
> Ms Ampadu, a black bar worker, was very upset by the video
> which contained what the tribunal said was racist material.
> Although the landlord had not played the video to harass
> Ms Ampadu, the tribunal ruled that it was race discrimination to
> make her work in the bar whilst the video was being played.

## An offensive working environment

### Nude pin-ups

In *Stewart* v *Cleveland Guest (Engineering) Ltd* [1994] IRLR 440 the
EAT recognised that the display of nude pictures in the workplace may,
in some cases, constitute sexual harassment and therefore sex discrimination. However in that particular case, the EAT refused to make a
finding of sex discrimination on the ground that the pictures of nude and
semi-nude women might have been just as offensive to a man as to
Ms Stewart.

The EAT conceded that this may be an area in which there is no correct
answer. However, it added that, in most cases, if not all, it should be
possible, by a combination of sensitivity and common sense, to arrange
matters so that the reasonable wishes of all concerned are accommodated.

The EAT's decision in the *Stewart* case has been widely criticised. It is
very possible that the decision will not be followed in the future, and that
a court will rule that the display of nude or similar pictures in the
workplace does amount to discrimination against one sex, even if members of the opposite sex are also offended. The sensible course of action
for employers is to prohibit nude pin-ups.

### Office banter

The EC Code of Practice provides that creating an offensive working
environment may be classed as sexual harassment. The same principles
apply to harassment on the grounds of race and disability.

Employers must ensure that conversations with offensive sexual and
racial overtones or which denigrate disabled people, which may be
regarded by some as "office banter" and part of the acceptable routine of
life in the workplace, do not become offensive and unwanted.

### Example

Whilst a female employee might be happy to join in conversations
with sexual innuendo, personal remarks by her colleagues about
her private sexual practices may be regarded by her as offensive,
therefore amounting to sexual harassment.

## Harassment as discrimination

Harassment may amount to direct sex, race or disability discrimination against the victim (see Chapters 1, 2 and 3).

To establish discrimination contrary to the SDA, RRA or DDA, the victim of the harassment must first show that he or she has been treated less favourably than another person in the same or similar circumstances and that the difference in treatment was due to their sex, race or disability.

The courts have recognised that it is the nature of the victim's treatment which is important and not the motives of the perpetrator of the harassment.

---

### Example

If a woman is subjected to a campaign of abusive sexual remarks because she is unpopular with her colleagues, it is no defence to argue that an unpopular man would also have been treated unfavourably. This is because the treatment of a woman which contains a significant sexual element is regarded as treatment on the grounds of her sex. The treatment is a particular kind of weapon, based upon the sex of the victim, which would not be used against an equally disliked man (*Strathclyde Regional Council* v *Porcelli* [1986] IRLR 134).

---

In *Insitu Cleaning Co Ltd* v *Heads* (above), the company argued that a remark to a woman about the size of her breasts was not sex-related and could not therefore be sex discrimination. It claimed that a similar remark could have been made to a man about his balding head. The EAT said that this argument was "absurd", as a remark about a woman's breasts is clearly sexual, whilst a remark about a man's bald head is not.

In the same way, any harassment which has a racial element will be treated as being on the grounds of race, regardless of the perpetrator's motives.

---

### Examples

If a black employee is subjected to racial abuse by his colleagues because he is unpopular, it is no defence to argue that a white employee who was unpopular would also be treated unfavourably. The victim's treatment contains a racial element because of his race, and this particular form of treatment would not be used against an equally disliked white employee.

In *McAuley* v *Auto Alloys Foundry Ltd* and Another COIT 62824/93 Mr McAuley – an Irishman – was the butt of comments from his colleagues, such as, that he was a 'typical thick paddy'. When Mr McAuley was dismissed he brought a successful claim for race discrimination. The tribunal found that the comments by his colleagues amounted to less favourable treatment on the ground of race. Mr McAuley's employers were liable because they had not taken steps to deal with the problem following complaints by Mr McAuley.

## Detriment

Having established that he or she has been treated less favourably on the grounds of sex, race or disability, the victim still has to show that he or she has suffered a detriment as a result of the harassment. Detriment could be dismissal, denial of opportunities within or for employment, or any other detriment – s 6(2) SDA, s 6(2) RRA, s 4(2)(d) DDA. Examples of detriment other than dismissal include: disciplinary action, denial of benefits and bonuses, being overlooked for promotion and being forced to resign. The victim has to show that the detriment was caused by the harassment, although in many cases the link between the two will be obvious, *e.g.* where a highly competent employee is demoted after rejecting a sexual proposal by her manager.

The victim may still have a good claim where the detrimental treatment follows from his or her own actions.

### Example

A woman is indecently touched at an office party by a friend of her employer and she retaliates by pouring a drink over him. She is sacked shortly afterwards without a proper explanation. The dismissal may amount to sex discrimination, because a male employee would not have been harassed that way in the first place (*Walsh* v *William Rutter Management Holdings Ltd* COIT 11404/41).

Even if the victim's employment status and opportunities are unaffected by the harassment, the act of harassment itself is likely to constitute a detriment. "Detriment" simply means that the victim has been put at a disadvantage (*Insitu Cleaning Co Ltd* v *Heads* [1995] IRLR 4).

## Liability of employers for acts of abuse and harassment by their employees

An employer is liable for the discriminatory acts of its employees when the acts are done in the course of the employee's employment, whether or not the acts are done with the employer's knowledge or approval (ss 32(1) RRA, 41(1) SDA and 58(1) DDA).

Whether an act is done in the course of the employee's employment will depend on the acts which the employer has authorised the employee to do. If the employee's conduct is a mode (albeit an improper one) of doing an authorised act, the employee will be acting in the course of his or her employment and the employer may be liable.

### Example

In *Bracebridge Engineering Ltd* v *Darby* [1990] IRLR 3 a woman was indecently assaulted by two supervisors after they had accused her of leaving work early. The EAT ruled that the supervisors had acted in the course of their employment as they were carrying out their authorised duties, albeit in an unauthorised manner.

However if the employee's actions do not form part of his or her duties, and the only connection they have with the employment is the fact that they are done in the workplace or during working hours, they will not be done in the course of employment and the employer will not be liable for them.

**Example**

In *Irving* v *The Post Office* [1987] IRLR 289 a postman had written racially abusive comments on the post delivered to individuals on his "round". The Court of Appeal ruled that this was not an act done in the course of the postman's employment, as he was acting outside of his duties when he wrote on the mail he was delivering. As a result the Post Office was not liable for the postman's actions.

## Minimising the risk of claims arising from employees' acts

Employers may not be held liable for the acts of their employees if the employer took all such steps as are reasonably practicable to prevent their employees from doing the discriminatory acts. The burden of proof is on the employer to show that he has taken such steps, which could include for example:

- having an equal opportunities or harassment policy (see Appendices 1 and 2);

- issuing disciplinary procedures which make clear that acts of racial or sexual abuse or harassment or abuse or harassment of a person with a disability will be treated as acts of gross misconduct which could give rise to summary dismissal of the offending employee;

- drawing employees attention to the above at periodic intervals and explaining their importance;

- arranging training in the meaning of "equal opportunities".

If an employer wants to avoid claims for discrimination it is not enough that an employer has an equal opportunities or harassment policy. The employer must take steps to ensure that the policy is:

- given to existing staff at the time of its introduction;

- given to new staff when they join;

- updated and implemented, *e.g.* by asking employees at staff meetings or at annual appraisals whether they understand the policy or have any questions about it, or have any complaints which might come within the ambit of the policy;

The policy should enable employees to approach a senior level of management in the first instance in cases where the harasser may be their immediate line manager.

## Liability of employers for acts of abuse and harassment by third parties

In *Burton* v *de Vere Hotels* [1996] IRLR 596 the EAT ruled that an employer was liable when racially offensive remarks were made by a third party to two black employees. The remarks were made by the comedian Bernard Manning who was appearing as after-dinner speaker at one of the employer's hotels. The hotel manager knew that Mr Manning's act was likely to include sexually explicit jokes, although he was not aware that Mr Manning was likely to say anything racist. The two employees, who were waitresses, were told by the manager to clear tables, which they did during Mr Manning's performance. When he saw the waitresses, Mr Manning made the remarks which upset the employees and encouraged other guests to join in with more abuse.

Although the hotel manager later apologised for what had happened, the employees brought claims against the employer for race discrimination. The EAT ruled that the employer was liable, even though the harassment was committed by a third party and not another employee. The EAT said that:

> "a person subjects another to something if he causes or allows that thing to happen in circumstances where he can control whether it happens or not. An employer subjects an employee to the detriment of racial harassment if he causes or permits the racial harassment to occur in circumstances in which he can control whether it happens or not".

The hotel manager failed to exercise proper control, when he could have told his assistants to monitor Mr Manning's performance and to remove the waitresses if the situation became unpleasant.

**Example**

Similarly, in *Go Kidz Ltd* v *Bourdouane* (EAT 1110/95) a company which organised children's parties on a commercial basis was liable to one of its employees who was sexually harassed by a parent at a party which she hosted. The parent had made a series of sexual remarks to Mrs Bourdouane, which prompted her to leave the party and complain to one of the company's directors. She described the parent's remarks as "perverted" and made it clear that she did not want to continue with the party, but the director encouraged her to return because all the other staff were occupied. The situation then became worse. The same parent continued to make offensive remarks, pressed himself against Ms Bourdouane whenever she walked past him, and finally pinched and smacked her bottom. The EAT upheld the tribunal's ruling that, once a complaint about the parent's behaviour had been made, the director should have taken steps to prevent Ms Bourdouane from being subjected to any further harassment. By failing to do so, the company, through the director, had discriminated against her.

## Steps to be taken by an employer when dealing with allegations of abuse or harassment

Full details of the complaint should be obtained by the employer from the alleged victim. If the victim is a female employee complaining of sexual harassment, the details should be taken either by a female manager or with a senior female employee in attendance.

A note of the details should be prepared and the victim should be asked to confirm that the facts are correctly stated in the note.

In a case of serious sexual or racial harassment the employer should consider suspending the harasser whilst an investigation is being carried out. It is advisable that the disciplinary procedure and/or contract of employment should contain a right for the employer to suspend employees whilst an investigation is being carried out.

The person accused of harassment should be asked to provide full details of their views on the act or acts complained of and should be asked to prepare a written statement. Usually it will be necessary to reveal the name of the accuser and this should be explained to the victim at the outset.

If there are discrepancies between the information given by the victim and the accused, then a disciplinary hearing should be held where the accused should be given a full opportunity to answer the allegations or otherwise justify or excuse the conduct complained of and the accused should be given an opportunity to produce witnesses at the disciplinary hearing.

Following the conclusion of the disciplinary hearing, careful consideration must be given to the penalty to be imposed. In serious cases of harassment, the likely outcome will be dismissal. In less serious cases, it may be appropriate to transfer the harasser or victim to other duties (if possible), or to give a written or final written warning.

## False claims of abuse or harassment

If, following a complaint of harassment and following the completion of an investigation under the grievance procedure, the employer has reason to believe that the complaint is unfounded or has been brought in bad faith then the employer should advise the alleged victim who complained of the abuse or harassment of the outcome of the investigation into their complaint.

The victim should then be told that, as the allegations appear to the employer to be unfounded or to have been brought in bad faith, the victim may have committed a disciplinary offence and that an investigation under the disciplinary procedure will follow.

If, following the outcome of the disciplinary procedure, the employer has reasonable grounds to believe that the victim's complaint was false or brought from a bad motive, then the employer should issue a formal warning or dismiss the employee.

In either case, once the disciplinary hearing has decided on the penalty to be imposed, the individual employee affected should have the right to appeal against the decision before it is implemented.

It is advisable that through all stages of the disciplinary and grievance procedure careful notes are taken of the evidence because it may be used in an industrial tribunal to establish the reasonableness or otherwise of the employer's conduct of the matter.

## Unfair constructive dismissal

In addition to any complaint to an industrial tribunal of discrimination that an employee may pursue against a fellow employee and against his employer, where the discrimination by an employer leads to an employee's resignation, then the employer's conduct in causing the employee to resign can form the basis of a claim for unfair constructive dismissal.

A constructive dismissal will arise where the employee terminates the employment with or without notice to the employer, in circumstances such that he is entitled to terminate the contract without notice by reason of the employer's conduct or by reason of the conduct of another employee for whose acts the employer will be vicariously liable. The employee must be able to show an industrial tribunal that the employer has committed a serious breach of contract or that the employer is no longer prepared to be bound by one or more of the express or implied terms of the contract of employment. The employee must also show that he has terminated the contract in response to the employer's breach of contract; and that he has not waived the breach by undue delay.

### Example

In *Melkonian* v *Zenith Engineering Ltd* COIT 26 May 1987 an employee resigned and accepted lower paid employment elsewhere as a direct result of racially offensive remarks made by fellow employees. Mr Melkonian alleged that he had been called a "black bastard" by the son of the managing director; was ostracised by other employees in the canteen; and had to endure offensive remarks from fellow employees. Mr Melkonian protested about these incidents to the managing director who warned employees that, if they were victimising Mr Melkonian, they were to stop it. The managing director took no more positive action. Eventually, Mr Melkonian decided to find another job and resigned his employment with Zenith in favour of a job which paid £50 less per week. The industrial tribunal ruled that because of the conduct of his employer and/or his fellow employees, Mr Melkonian had suffered racial discrimination and that as a direct result of that discrimination he had left his employment for other employment and was entitled to be compensated for his losses arising from the change of employment.

To minimise the risk of claims for unfair constructive dismissal, employers should:

- take all complaints of harassment seriously and should deal with them as set out above;
- interview employees who are seeking to resign to establish the true reasons for the employee's departure;
- if the employee indicates that he or she may have been the victim of harassment, then before accepting the employee's resignation, the employer should investigate the complaint and take disciplinary action against the offender if it is appropriate to do so;
- the employer should consider allowing the employee to take paid leave from work (if the employee wishes) whilst an investigation is undertaken;
- an employer's failure to investigate a complaint may itself give rise to a claim of discrimination.

**Summary**
**Harassment**

- Harassment is not defined in SDA, RRA or DDA, but can be described as unwanted conduct of a sexual or racial nature, or other conduct based on race or sex affecting the dignity of women and men at work.

- Harassment (even a single incident of harassment) can amount to direct sex, race or disability discrimination.

- Employers can be liable for acts of harassment committed by their employees and, in some cases, by third parties.

- Employers may avoid liability for their employee's acts if they take all such steps as are reasonably practical to prevent the discriminatory acts, for example, by having and implementing an equal opportunities or harassment policy (see Appendices 1 and 2).

- Complaints of harassment should be dealt with under the employer's disciplinary/ grievance procedure.

- An employer's failure to properly investigate a complaint could give rise to a claim for unfair constructive dismissal.

# CONTENTS OF CHAPTER 17

*Victimisation*

# 17.  VICTIMISATION

## Definition

For the statutory definition of "victimisation" in the RRA, SDA and DDA, see Chapters 1, 2 and 3.

Employers should recognise that many victims of race, sex and disability discrimination may be reluctant to bring proceedings, particularly against their own employer, where they fear that it may result in dismissal, denial of promotion or victimisation in some other way. The provisions of the RRA, SDA and DDA are designed to give some protection from such victimisation.

Employers will be acting unlawfully if they instruct an employee to discriminate and there would be a further act of discrimination if the employee then refused to carry out the act of discrimination and was then disciplined for so doing.

### Example

A manager is told not to promote an employee in his section on the grounds of that employee's race. The manager then refuses to comply with that request and seeks to promote the employee. The manager is then himself disciplined. In such a case, the manager could bring a claim for race discrimination.

In *Zarczynska* v *Levy* [1978] IRLR 532 a part-time barmaid was dismissed because she refused to obey an instruction that she must not serve black customers. The EAT ruled that the barmaid had received less favourable treatment on racial grounds than the treatment which would have been received by a barmaid prepared to obey the instructions.

## Avoiding claims of victimisation

Employers should give the clearest possible instructions to all employees that there must be no victimisation as a result of any formal or informal complaint of discrimination. The legislation protects from victimisation witnesses and potential witnesses as well as the victims themselves. Employers should note that no pressure of any kind must be used to persuade the victim not to proceed with the complaint or witnesses not to give evidence.

## Private households

Generally the RRA dos not apply to employment in a private household ( s 4(3) RRA). The exemption applies where the employment is genuinely in a private household and not for business purposes. The exemption under the RRA only applies to recruitment, employment and dismissal and does not apply to victimisation, nor does it apply to contract workers. This means that domestic staff supplied by an agency keep the right to complain of discrimination.

The SDA does not now contain a similar exemption. The equivalent provision, s (3)(a), was repealed by s 1(1) Sex Discrimination Act 1986.

## Disability discrimination

The DDA makes it unlawful to victimise disabled people who make use of, or try to make use of, their rights under the DDA. People who help disabled people complain about discrimination are also protected from being victimised or treated less favourably.

The DDA also protects those who:

• take an employer to a tribunal under the DDA;

• give evidence, or supply information in connection with proceedings under the DDA;

• help a disabled person who is covered by the DDA;

• alleges that someone has ignored the DDA's provisions;

• are believed to have done any of the above.

# CONTENTS OF CHAPTER 18

*Health and Safety*

# 18.  HEALTH AND SAFETY

## New or expectant mothers

Special protection is given to pregnant workers, those who have given birth within the last 6 months and to those who are breast-feeding. The relevant provisions are contained in ss 66–70 ERA and the Management of Health & Safety at Work (Amendment) Regulations 1994 (SI 1994/2865).

In addition to the duty to assess the health and safety risks in the workplace for all their employees, employers who employ women of child-bearing age must specifically assess the health and safety risks to new or expectant mothers. This risk assessment must be carried out even if there are no new or expectant mothers amongst the women of child-bearing age.

If a new or expectant mother is subject to any health and safety risk, *e.g.* because of the physical work she carries out or the substances she deals with, the employer must take all appropriate action to prevent the worker from being exposed to the risk. If necessary, and if reasonable to do so, the employer must alter the working hours and conditions of the employee in order to avoid the risk. If such changes are not reasonable or would not avoid the risk, the employee should be offered suitable alternative work until either the risk is removed or until the woman is no longer at risk.

If it is not possible either to change the working hours or conditions, or to offer suitable alternative work, then the employee must be suspended from work until she is no longer at risk. During the period of suspension, the employee must receive all of her contractual entitlements, including pay.

If a new or expectant mother unreasonably refuses an offer of suitable alternative work, she may be suspended without remuneration during the period of suspension.

The employer is not obliged to change the employee's working hours or conditions, offer her alternative work, or suspend her from work, unless he has received written notice that she is pregnant, that she has recently given birth or that she is breast-feeding.

If, having taken steps to avoid a risk, the employer is satisfied that the employee is no longer a new or expectant mother, he is no longer required to maintain those steps.

*Night work*

Where a new or expectant mother works at night, and she has a medical certificate stating that she should not work at night, the employer must offer her suitable alternative work. If no such work is available, the employee must be suspended from work on full pay for so long as is necessary for her health and safety.

## Compulsory maternity leave

The Maternity (Compulsory Leave) Regulations 1994 (SI 1994/2479) provide that employees who are entitled to maternity leave are not allowed to work during the period of 2 weeks following the birth of their child. The prohibition is enforced by the Health & Safety Executive or local authorities. Employers who fail to comply and permit women to work during the two-week period are liable to prosecution and a fine up to a current maximum of £500.

# CONTENTS OF CHAPTER 19

*Maternity and Paternity Rights*

# 19. MATERNITY AND PATERNITY RIGHTS

## Maternity rights

In this chapter we examine the special rights given to women in connection with pregnancy and childbirth. These are:

- time off with pay for antenatal care;
- statutory maternity leave;
- the right to return to work after maternity leave; and
- unfair dismissal rights.

It is specifically stated in s 2(2) SDA that the provision of these rights to women does not constitute sex discrimination against men.

This chapter also examines claims by women for sex discrimination in relation to pregnancy and maternity leave, and a man's entitlement to paternity leave.

For a maternity policy see Appendix 3.

## Antenatal care

### Right to paid time off

Pregnant employees, regardless of their length of service and the hours that they work each week, have the following rights in relation to antenatal care:

- the right not to be unreasonably refused time off work to attend antenatal care appointments (s 55(1)ERA); and
- the right to be paid for such absence at the appropriate hourly rate (s 56(1) ERA).

### Qualifying conditions

The following conditions have to be met for the employee to qualify for the above-mentioned rights:

- she must be pregnant;

- she must have made an appointment to receive antenatal care on the advice of a registered medical practitioner, registered midwife or registered health visitor;

- for the second and subsequent appointments she must, (if requested to do so by her employer), produce a certificate stating that she is pregnant from a doctor, midwife or health visitor and an appointment card or other document showing that the appointment has been made.

## What constitutes "antenatal care"?

There is no statutory definition of antenatal care, but it is likely to include appointments to see doctors and midwives, antenatal relaxation classes and parent-craft classes. It may also include an appointment made by a pregnant woman to see whether she is pregnant in the first place.

## What time off is allowed?

The woman's right is to time off during working hours. There is no requirement for her to make up for lost time, either by rearranging her hours of work or by coming into work on one of her days off (*Edgar* v *Giorgione Inns Ltd*, unreported – COIT 1803/13).

An employer may be able to claim that it is reasonable to refuse time off in certain circumstances. In *Gregory* v *Tudsbury Ltd* [1982] IRLR 267 an industrial tribunal suggested that it might be reasonable for an employer to refuse time off work if the employee could reasonably have made an appointment outside normal working hours. The tribunal did not provide examples of situations where an employer's refusal to allow time off would be reasonable. However it could, for example, be argued that an employee who only works for one or two afternoons per week should make appointments outside of her working hours, provided that the appointments are not urgent and that out of hours appointments are available.

If the employer does allow the employee to take time off, the employee is entitled to be paid. This applies even if the employer could reasonably have refused the time off but chose to allow it anyway (*Gregory* v *Tudsbury Ltd* above).

The employee is only allowed to take the time off which is needed to travel to and from, and to attend, the antenatal appointment.

> **Example**
>
> In *Gough* v *Country Sport (Wales) Ltd* COIT 2061/67 an employee
> who had an afternoon antenatal appointment took the morning off
> as well so that she could go to the hairdressers. She was dismissed
> by her employer, and the tribunal found that she could not claim
> sex discrimination because she was dismissed because of her mis-
> conduct and not because of her pregnancy.

## The employee's remedy

If an employee is unreasonably refused time off, or if she is allowed time off
but is not paid for all or part of that time, she can complain to an industrial
tribunal provided she does so within 3 months beginning on the date of the
relevant appointment. If the tribunal finds the complaint to be well founded,
it will make a declaration to that effect and will award compensation
equivalent to the sum which the employee would have received if she had
been allowed time off or if she had been paid for time taken.

## Statutory maternity leave

### Right to maternity leave

Until 1994, women only qualified for statutory maternity leave if they had
2 years' continuous service at the beginning of the eleventh week before
the expected week of childbirth (EWC).

Following changes to UK law in 1994, which were introduced to
comply with the EC Pregnant Workers' Directive (No. 92/85), there is
now a two-tier system of maternity leave as follows:

### Basic maternity leave

All pregnant employees, regardless of length of service or hours worked
per week, are entitled to statutory maternity leave of 14 weeks (referred
to in this chapter as "basic maternity leave") (s 73(1) ERA).

## Extended maternity leave

Employees who have at least 2 years' continuous service at the beginning of the eleventh week before the EWC are entitled to maternity leave of up to 40 weeks (referred to in this chapter as "extended maternity leave").

The ERA does not expressly provide for a forty-week leave period; rather it states that the employee may commence her leave up to 11 weeks before the EWC (s 74(2) ERA), and that she has a right to return to work up to 29 weeks after the start of the week in which the birth actually occurs (s 79 ERA).

## The expected week of childbirth

The EWC is defined in s 235(1) ERA as "the week beginning with midnight between Saturday and Sunday, in which it is expected that childbirth will occur".

The eleventh week before the EWC also begins with a Sunday, so to calculate the beginning of the eleventh week before the EWC, find the Sunday at the start of the EWC and count back 11 Sundays.

### Example

If the expected date of childbirth is Tuesday 11 November 1997, the EWC begins on Sunday 9 November 1997 and the eleventh week before the EWC begins on Sunday 24 August 1996. Thus if the employee has at least 2 years' continuous service by 24 August 1997, she will be able to take extended maternity leave, otherwise she will only be entitled to basic maternity leave.

## Notice provisions

In order to take maternity leave an employee must comply with certain notice provisions, depending on whether she intends to take basic or extended maternity leave.

If the employee fails to comply with these provisions she will lose her right to maternity leave.

## Basic maternity leave

To take basic maternity leave the employee must:

- Inform her employer in writing at least 21 days before her maternity leave begins (or as soon as is reasonably practicable) of the fact that she is pregnant and the EWC or, if childbirth has already occurred, the date of birth (s 75(1) ERA).

- Give her employer at least 21 days' notice (or as much notice as is reasonably practicable) of the date on which she wants her maternity leave to begin (s 74(1) ERA). This notice must be in writing if the employer so requests.

- If requested to do so by her employer, produce a certificate from a registered medical practitioner or a registered midwife stating the EWC (s 75(2) ERA).

## Extended maternity leave

To take extended maternity leave, the employee must first comply with the notification provisions for basic maternity leave set out above.

In addition she must inform her employer in writing at least 21 days before her maternity leave begins (or as soon as reasonably practicable) that she wishes to take extended maternity leave (s 80(1) ERA).

Having complied with the requirements before taking extended maternity leave, the employee must satisfy further notification provisions during her leave in order to be able to return to work. These are dealt with below.

## When can maternity leave begin?

The employee is generally free to choose when her maternity leave will begin, provided that:

- the earliest it can begin is the start of the eleventh week before the EWC (s 74(2) ERA); and

- the latest it can begin is the actual date of birth (s 72(2) ERA).

## Triggering of maternity leave

Regardless of the date chosen by the employee for the beginning of her maternity leave, the maternity leave period will automatically be triggered if:

• Childbirth occurs before the maternity leave was due to commence (s 72(2) ERA). Childbirth is defined as the birth of a living child or the birth of a child whether living or dead after 24 weeks' pregnancy (s 235(1) ERA).

• The employee is absent from work wholly or partly because of pregnancy or childbirth after the start of the sixth week before the EWC (s 72(1)(b) ERA).

An employee who is absent for only one day due to a pregnancy-related illness during the 6 weeks before the EWC is likely to have her maternity leave triggered. It is even arguable that an employee who is absent for part of the day will come within this provision (*e.g.* an employee who is late arriving at work due to morning sickness). However, the provision does not apply to time taken off work to attend antenatal appointments, or suspension from work on health and safety grounds (Chapter 18).

It may be difficult in some cases to determine whether an absence is due to pregnancy, particularly where an employee has an illness or condition which may be due to other reasons, *e.g.* high blood pressure. The DSS Benefits Agency has published a booklet called "Pregnancy Related Illness" which provides some guidance on the likely connection of many conditions with pregnancy.

There is nothing to prevent employers waiving days of pregnancy-related absence so that maternity leave is not automatically triggered by s 72(1)(b) ERA.

## Giving notice when maternity leave is triggered

If maternity leave is automatically triggered, an employee who has not already done so will be unable to give notice of her intention to take leave. The legislation provides for this as follows:

• where childbirth occurs before leave begins or before notice of leave is given by the employee, the woman must notify her employer that she has given birth as soon as is reasonably practicable (s 74(5) ERA).

- where leave is triggered because the employee is absent from work wholly or partly because of pregnancy or childbirth after the beginning of the sixth week before the EWC, she must notify her employer as soon as is reasonably practicable that she is absent for that reason (s 74(4) ERA).

In both cases notice must be given in writing if the employer so requests.

## Employees' benefits during maternity leave

### Basic maternity leave

All contractual terms and conditions, except those relating to remuneration (see below), are expressly preserved during the basic maternity leave (s 71 ERA).

### Remuneration

Employees who take only basic maternity leave are entitled to all their normal contractual benefits except for remuneration throughout their leave. Remuneration is not defined in the legislation, but it is likely to include contractual bonuses and commission as well as wages and salary.

---

**Example**

In *Gillespie v Northern Health and Social Services Board* [1996] IRLR 214 Mrs Gillespie challenged the remuneration exception in s 71 ERA and claimed sex discrimination on the basis that she had not received full pay during maternity leave. The case was referred to the ECJ who rejected her claims, and ruled that the principles of equal pay and equal treatment under European Community law (see Chapter 14) do not require that women should continue to receive full pay during maternity leave. However if a bonus which is paid during an employee's maternity leave relates to a period when the employee was at work, she may be able to claim a proportion of it.

## Benefits in kind

Benefits in kind (*e.g.* company cars, membership of clubs) are not classed as remuneration and therefore the employee is entitled to receive these during her basic maternity leave.

## Holidays, pension benefits and share schemes

As the contract is preserved during basic maternity leave, employers must also allow employees to accrue holidays, receive employer's pension contributions, accrue service for promotion and participate in share schemes as if they were not on maternity leave.

If an employee resigns during basic maternity leave, she is entitled to receive her benefits up to the date on which her employment comes to an end.

## Extended maternity leave

For the first 14 weeks of extended maternity leave, the position is the same as for women who take basic maternity leave, *i.e.* all normal contractual benefits (except remuneration – see above) are preserved.

The position is different beyond the first 14 weeks of extended maternity leave, because the legislation does not expressly preserve contractual terms during this period.

Following the decisions of the EAT in *Institute of the Motor Industry* v *Harvey* [1992] ICR 470 and *Hilton International Hotels (UK) Ltd* v *Kaissi* [1994] IRLR 270 it seemed that contractual terms would be preserved beyond the first 14 weeks unless the contract was terminated by agreement, resignation or dismissal.

However, in *Crouch* v *Kidsons Impey* [1996] IRLR 79 the EAT ruled that the contract is not presumed to continue after the first 14 weeks. Whether or not the contract does continue depends on whether such continuation was expressly or impliedly agreed by the employer and employee.

If the contract is deemed to continue, the employee will be entitled to the same benefits as during the first 14 weeks of her leave, unless the contract expressly provides otherwise.

## Continuity of service during maternity leave

An employee's continuous service with her employer determines many of her statutory rights, *e.g.* the right to claim unfair dismissal and redundancy payments, the minimum period of notice to which she is entitled on dismissal, and, of course, her entitlement to maternity leave. Different rules apply depending on whether the employee is taking basic or extended maternity leave.

### *Basic maternity leave*

As the contract is expressly preserved during basic maternity leave (s 71 ERA), continuity of service is also preserved and the period of absence counts towards the employee's continuous service with her employer.

### *Extended maternity leave*

If the employee returns to work after extended maternity leave having complied with the statutory provisions, continuity is preserved and each week of her absence counts towards her continuous service with her employer (s 212(2)–(4) ERA).

If the employee has failed to comply with the statutory requirements for returning to work, her continuity will still be preserved if her contract has continued throughout her extended leave.

If the employee has neither a statutory nor a contractual right to return to work, her continuity will only be preserved if she returns to work after not more than 26 weeks' absence.

### Example

In *Mitchell* v *Royal British Legion Club* [1981] ICR 18 Ms Mitchell was allowed to take time off work to have a baby although she did not comply with the statutory notice requirements as neither she nor the club were aware of her maternity rights. She returned to work after 16 weeks' leave, but was dismissed 2 days later. Although Ms Mitchell had not had a statutory or contractual right to return to work, her continuity of service was preserved during her absence because she had returned within 26 weeks, and as a result she was able to pursue a claim for unfair dismissal.

## Maternity pay

Although an employee has no right to contractual remuneration during maternity leave, she may qualify for maternity allowance or statutory maternity pay, depending on her length of service with the employer and her national insurance contributions.

## Returning from maternity leave

The rules relating to notice provisions are different depending on whether the employee is returning from basic or extended maternity leave.

### *Returning from basic maternity leave*

Having complied with the notice provisions before taking her maternity leave, an employee does not have to confirm to her employer that she intends to return to work from basic maternity leave – she simply has to turn up for work at the end of the 14 weeks. This is because her contract continues throughout the fourteen-week period.

If, however, the employee wishes to return before the end of the fourteen-week period, she must give her employer 7 days' notice of the date on which she intends to return (s 76 ERA). If she fails to give this notice, the employer can postpone her return to a date which will ensure that she has given 7 days' notice, although the employee's return cannot be delayed beyond the end of the fourteen-week period. If the employee still turns up for work early despite such postponement of her return by her employer, the employer does not have to remunerate her until sufficient notice has been given or the fourteen-week period has expired, whichever is sooner.

## Returning from extended maternity leave

An employee who wishes to return from extended maternity leave must comply with certain notification procedures, which are additional to those which apply before taking leave.

Where an employee has indicated that she intends to take extended maternity leave, her employer may request written confirmation from her that she intends to return to work after her extended maternity leave (s 80(2) ERA).

The employer's request must be in writing and can be made not earlier than 21 days before the end of the first 14 weeks of leave. It must tell the employee that she has to give this confirmation in writing within 14 days, and that if she fails to do so she will lose her right to return to work from extended maternity leave.

If the employee receives such a request from her employer, she must give the confirmation in writing within 14 days (or as soon as is reasonably practicable) if she wants to return from extended maternity leave.

---

### Example

In *Betham* v *Alfa Romeo (Great Britain) Ltd* (unreported – COIT 1742/121), the employee confirmed her intention to return to work but did so after 17 days. Although the employer did not suffer any inconvenience as a result of the employee's delay in replying, the employee lost her statutory right to return as she had not responded within 14 days, and nothing had prevented her from doing so.

---

In addition to replying to any request for confirmation that she intends to return, the employee has a separate requirement to notify her employer in writing at least 21 days in advance of the date on which she intends to return to work (s 82(1) ERA). The date given by the employee is called the "notified date of return" (NDR).

If the employee fails to comply with either of the notice requirements, she will lose her statutory right to return to work. However she may still have a contractual right to return if her contract is deemed to continue beyond the first 14 weeks of her leave.

**Example**

In *Crouch* v *Kidson's Impey* (above) Ms Crouch had not complied with the notification procedures for taking extended maternity leave. Her employer nevertheless allowed her to leave work in March 1993 and paid her maternity pay up to 30 September 1993. In November 1993 Ms Crouch gave notice that she wished to return to work the following month, but her employer said that she had lost the right to return because she had failed to give the required notices before her leave commenced. Ms Crouch claimed unfair dismissal, and because she had no statutory right to return, the question was whether she had a contractual right, which depended on her contract having continued throughout her leave. The EAT stated that there is no presumption that the contract does continue after the first 14 weeks of extended maternity leave; it is a question of what was agreed by the parties. In this case the EAT ruled that the contract terminated by consent on 30 September when maternity pay ceased to be paid, and as a result Ms Crouch had no contractual right to return to work.

## Postponement of the return to work

### Extension of maternity leave when the birth is late

If a woman who is only entitled to basic maternity leave has exhausted her 14 week entitlement before her child is born, her leave is automatically extended until the birth of the child (s 73(1) ERA). She will also be prevented from returning to work within 2 weeks after the birth (see below). During this extra period of leave the woman is entitled to the same benefits as during the first 14 weeks of her leave.

### Prohibition on working within 2 weeks after the birth

The Maternity (Compulsory Leave) Regulations 1994 (SI 1994/2479) provide that employees who are entitled to maternity leave are not allowed to work during the period of 2 weeks following the birth of their child. The prohibition is enforced by the Health & Safety Executive or Local Authorities. Employers who fail to comply and permit women to work during the two-week period are liable to prosecution and a fine up to a current maximum of £500.

## Protection from dismissal

This is governed by s 99(3) ERA. If an employee is unable to return after maternity leave because of illness or disease, she may be protected from dismissal if she provides a doctor's certificate stating that she is unable to return. The protection lasts for the 4 weeks immediately following the end of her maternity leave, or for as long as the medical certificate is current, whichever is the shorter. If the employee is dismissed during the protected period, the dismissal will automatically be unfair.

## Postponement of return on medical grounds after extended maternity leave

Employees who qualify for extended maternity leave may postpone their return to work for up to 4 weeks from the notified date of return (NDR) (or from the end of the 29 weeks which start with the week of birth if the NDR has yet to be given) (s 82(3) ERA).

The employee must be incapable of working due to disease or mental or bodily disablement, although this need not relate to pregnancy or childbirth. The employee must produce a doctor's certificate to this effect before the NDR or before the end of the 29 week period from the birth if she has not yet given an NDR (s 82(4) ERA). If the employee does not provide a doctor's certificate, or if she fails to do so in time, she will lose her right to return to work (*Mearis* v *IMI Yorkshire Imperial Ltd* COIT 1408/60).

An employee can postpone her return on medical grounds only once (s 82(5) ERA), so if she is still too ill to go back to work after the first postponement, she will lose her statutory right to return. She may still however have a contractual right to return (see above).

## Postponement due to interruption of work

An employee returning from extended maternity leave may postpone her return where there is an interruption of work (*e.g.* a strike) which makes it unreasonable to expect her to return.

Where the employee has given an NDR, she may postpone her return until work resumes or as soon as reasonably practicable afterwards (s 82(6) ERA). The employee is not required to give a new NDR.

If the employee has yet to give an NDR, and an interruption of work makes it unreasonable to expect her to return before the end of the twenty-nine-week period from birth, she may give her employer an NDR which is not more than 28 days from the end of the interruption (s 82(7) ERA). However, the employee must still give 21 days' notice of the NDR.

If the employee is also entitled to postpone her return on medical grounds (see above), she can apply both provisions consecutively.

## Postponement by the employer

An employer may postpone an employee's return before the end of her basic maternity leave if she has not complied with s 76(1) ERA and given at least 7 days' notice of the date on which she intends to return (see above).

An employer may postpone an employee's return from extended maternity leave by up to 4 weeks from her NDR for any "specified reasons" (s 82(2) ERA). The employer must notify the employee before the NDR of the due date on which she will be entitled to return to work. This notice need not be in writing. There is no definition of "specified reasons" in the legislation. However, in *Stevens* v *Swanscombe and Greenhithe Town Council* COIT 1658/185 the tribunal said that "specified reasons" could include the council's general business requirements and were not restricted to matters connected with the employee's maternity leave.

## The employee's rights on returning to work

The general rule is that the employee must be allowed to return to her original job on terms and conditions not less favourable than those which would have applied to her if she had not been absent from work.

For employees returning from basic maternity leave, this right follows from the fact that their contracts are deemed to continue throughout their leave by s 71 ERA. For employees returning from extended maternity leave, the right to return is expressly set out in s 79 ERA.

If the employer does not comply with this right there will, in most circumstances, be a dismissal (see below). The employee may also be able to claim sex discrimination.

## Returning to the same job

To determine whether the employee is being allowed to return to the same job, it is necessary to consider the nature of the work which she is employed to do in accordance with her contract, and the capacity and place in which she is employed.

## What work is the employee employed to do?

The work which the employee is employed to do under her contract may be wider than the work which she actually did before her maternity leave.

### Example

In *Houghton* v *May and Hassell Ltd* COIT 837/180 Ms Houghton was employed as a general clerk and worked in the company's wages office. On her return from maternity leave she was offered jobs as a clerk in the sales and transport offices instead, but she refused them and claimed unfair dismissal. As she was employed as a general clerk and not as a wages clerk, the tribunal decided that she had been offered work which she was contractually employed to do, and the company had therefore complied with its obligations.

## Capacity

The employee's capacity includes her status in the work place. Even if the job which she is offered on her return comes within her contract, the employer will not comply with its obligations if her status is lower than before.

### Example

In *Taylor* v *Staffordshire Building Society* COIT 1326/50 the employee had, before taking maternity leave, been the managing director's secretary, with an office on the top executive floor of the building and with confidential work. On her return, she was asked to work for the manager of the premises department, which involved working in the basement and refilling the ladies' sanitary machines. Although the new position came within the work which she was contractually employed to do, and her pay and other benefits had not been reduced, the tribunal held that her capacity and status had been reduced and she was not therefore being offered the same job.

## The place of work

Unless the employee's contract contains a mobility clause (see Chapter 22), the employee must be allowed to return to the place where she worked before taking maternity leave. If the employer does not allow her to return to her old workplace, this is likely to be a dismissal, even if the employee is allowed to do the same work as before taking maternity leave.

The employer may however be able to show a valid reason why it is not possible for the employee to return to her old workplace, so that any dismissal will be fair.

### Example

Whilst an employee is absent on maternity leave, her employer closes down its factory and moves to a larger factory two miles away so that it can cope with a necessary increase in production. On returning from her leave, the employee is offered the same work but at the new factory. The employee's contract does not contain a mobility clause, and she refuses to work at the new factory and claims unfair dismissal. The employer can rely on the need for larger premises as a valid reason for the change in the place of work and a fair reason for the dismissal.

However if the work which the employee does is still available at her old place of work, she must be allowed to return there. In particular, the employer cannot claim that the work is not availableat the old work place because someone else is now doing the employee's job.

> **Example**
>
> In *Huth* v *Davidsons* COIT 1409/223 Ms Huth, who worked for a firm of solicitors, was asked to work in a different office several miles away on her return from maternity leave, because her job at her previous office was being done by someone else. A tribunal decided that the firm's refusal to re-employ Ms Huth at her old place of work amounted to unfair dismissal.

## Terms and conditions on returning to work

Having allowed the employee to return to the same job, the employer must ensure that her terms and conditions of employment are no less favourable than they would have been if she had not been absent on maternity leave.

If the employee's terms are less favourable, she may be able to resign and claim unfair constructive dismissal (see Chapter 16) if she is returning from basic maternity leave. If the employee is returning from extended maternity leave, there will be a "deemed" dismissal under s 96(1) ERA (see below). The employee may also be able to claim sex discrimination.

The employee must be allowed to benefit from any improvements to her terms and conditions which have taken place during her leave.

> **Example**
>
> If the employer gives all employees a 5 per cent pay rise whilst a woman is on maternity leave, her salary on returning to work must reflect this increase.

Where pay increases are given on an individual basis to reflect an employee's performance during the year, an employee who has been on maternity leave for part of the year appears to be at a disadvantage. It would be advisable for the employer to account for this by examining such an employee's performance during the months whilst she was at work, and extrapolating the figures to produce an assessment for a full working year.

### Example

A saleswoman takes 6 months' maternity leave up to the end of her employer's financial year. Her contract provides for percentage increases in salary at the end of each financial year depending upon her total sales during the year. If her sales during the 6 months whilst she is at work amount to £100,000, the employer could assess her salary increase on an annual sales total of £200,000, so that when the employee returns to work, she will have benefited from the increase in salary as if she had not been absent.

The above example is obviously simple, and the employer may be able (or obliged) to account for seasonal differences in performance when assessing pay increases for employees who are or have been on maternity leave. It may even be possible for the employee to claim that her performance during the months when she was at work was affected by her pregnancy or recent childbirth, and that allowances should be made accordingly.

An employee returning from maternity leave will also be affected by any changes to her terms and conditions made during her leave which are to her disadvantage.

### Example

Whilst an employee is on maternity leave, her colleagues agree with the employer to an increase in their hours of work. When the woman returns to work the new hours will apply to her, as they would have done if she had not been on maternity leave.

## Returning to work part-time

Many women returning from maternity leave will want to change their hours of work or work part-time instead of full-time. Some employees may have contracts which expressly allow them to do this.

Employees who are not in this position may however be able to claim sex discrimination if their employer refuses to allow the change. Any claim for sex discrimination in these circumstances will be a claim for indirect sex discrimination (Chapter 2), on the basis that:

- the employer is applying a requirement to both men and women that they work certain hours;

- the proportion of women who can comply with the requirement is considerably smaller than the proportion of men who can comply, because women are more likely to have child care responsibilities;

- the requirement is to the woman's detriment because she cannot comply with it; and

- the requirement is not justifiable on non-sex grounds.

Whether or not the employer's refusal amounts to sex discrimination is likely to turn on the question of justifiability, and in most cases it will be very difficult for the employer to justify its requirement.

It is not sufficient for the employer to claim that any change in the employee's hours would be inconvenient or too expensive for the business. What an employer has to show is that the requirement is necessary and appropriate to achieve the needs of the business, and this will depend on, amongst other things, the nature and size of the business and the nature of the employee's work.

## Example

A receptionist who worked full-time before taking maternity leave wants to work for only 3 days of the week on her return, which means that the employer would also have to employ one or more other receptionists on a part-time basis. Due to the nature of the job, the employer cannot argue that it is necessary to have one full-time rather than two or more part-time receptionists. As a result, the employer's refusal to allow the employee to work part-time would be indirect sex discrimination.

In some cases the employer may be able to argue that the particular job could not be done properly if shared by two or more people working part-time.

**Examples**

In *Clymo* v *Wandsworth LBC* [1989] IRLR 241 a branch librarian wanted to job-share on her return from maternity leave. The council refused, and the EAT ruled that there was no discrimination. The requirement that the employee work full-time could be justified because her job involved management responsibility and could not be done properly on a job-share basis, unlike a more junior position where job-sharing was permitted by the council.

In *Bell* v *East Kilbride Development Corporation* SCOIT S/1335/91 a senior finance assistant in the accounts department wanted to return to work on a part-time basis. The employer argued that the preparation of monthly accounts required a high level of continuity which could not be achieved with part-time workers or job-sharers, and that if such an arrangement was allowed there would be a greater risk of mistakes. The tribunal accepted the employer's evidence and held that its requirement was not discriminatory.

By way of contrast is *Puttick* v *Eastbourne BC* COIT 316-2 where a refusal to allow a clerical worker in the council's tax department to job share was found to be discriminatory. The council had claimed that a job share would be inefficient as one worker would have to spend time updating the other when the job was handed over during the week; members of the public would be confused as they would not be certain which worker was dealing with their case; and the training costs for the job would effectively be doubled. The tribunal rejected these arguments and ruled that the requirement to work full-time was not justifiable. The work was allocated on a rota system, the job did not involve any serious decision making, and there was no reason why job-sharing arrangements could not have been made.

In *British Telecommunications plc* v *Roberts* (EAT 315/95) an industrial tribunal ruled that the refusal to allow two women returning from maternity leave to job-share was direct sex discrimination, as it was a direct consequence of their pregnancies (see below). The EAT overturned this decision, ruling that the employees' complaint was connected with their child care responsibilities and not their pregnancies. There was therefore no direct sex discrimination, although the EAT remitted the case to the tribunal to determine whether the employer's refusal amounted to indirect discrimination.

## Unfair dismissal and maternity leave

### Dismissal prior to maternity leave

If a woman is dismissed before her maternity leave begins, she will lose the right to take leave and return to work afterwards. Provided she has sufficient continuous service she can pursue an ordinary claim for unfair dismissal. If the dismissal is for a reason connected with her pregnancy, she can claim automatically unfair dismissal under s 99 ERA even if she has less than 2 years' service, and also sex discrimination.

### Dismissal during maternity leave

#### Basic maternity leave

If a woman is dismissed during basic maternity leave, her maternity leave and her contract end with the dismissal (s 73(3) ERA) and she cannot return to work. Provided the woman has 2 years' continuous service, she will be able to pursue an ordinary unfair dismissal claim or a claim for redundancy. The outcome will depend on the reason for the dismissal.

Regardless of her length of service, the woman may be able to show that the dismissal was automatically unfair under s 99 ERA if it was for a reason connected with her pregnancy or childbirth, or if she is redundant and she has not been offered a suitable vacancy (see below).

#### Extended maternity leave

The effect of an attempt to dismiss a woman during extended maternity leave depends on whether her contract is continuing at the time. This is because an employee cannot actually be dismissed when her contract is not continuing.

If the woman is dismissed during the first 14 weeks, or if she is dismissed during the extended period where her contract is deemed to continue beyond 14 weeks, the dismissal will bring the contract to an end.

The woman may have ordinary claims for unfair dismissal and redundancy, as well as for automatically unfair dismissal, depending on the reason for the dismissal.

The dismissal does not however prevent the woman from exercising her statutory right to return to work from extended maternity leave under s 79 ERA because such a right does not depend on the continuation of her contract. If the woman does return to work under her statutory right, she must repay any compensation she has received for unfair dismissal or redundancy if requested to do so by her employer (s 84 ERA).

If the employer tries to dismiss the woman after the first 14 weeks where her contract is not deemed to continue, the employer's attempted dismissal will have no effect because the employee cannot actually be dismissed when she does not have a contract. The woman will still have a statutory right to return to work if she complies with the proper notice provisions, and if the employer does not take her back there will be a "deemed" dismissal under s 96(1) ERA on her notified date of return.

## What happens if an employer denies a woman her right to return to work?

### Refusal amounting to dismissal

A woman's right to return to the same job after her maternity leave has been discussed above. If the employer does not comply with this right, either by refusing to let her return at all or by offering her a different job, the refusal will normally amount to a dismissal. The fairness of the dismissal will depend on the reasons behind it.

If the woman is returning from basic maternity leave, or from extended maternity leave where her contract has continued throughout her leave, the employer's refusal will bring her contract to an end and the dismissal will be an ordinary unfair dismissal under s 95 ERA. Provided the woman has sufficient continuous service she will be able to pursue an ordinary unfair dismissal or redundancy claim in the usual way. Regardless of her length of service she may also have claims for automatically unfair dismissal and sex discrimination.

If the woman is exercising her statutory right to return from extended maternity leave under s 79 ERA where her contract has not continued, then (subject to the exceptions under s 96(2), (3) ERA set out below) the refusal will be a deemed dismissal under s 96(1) ERA. This special provision applies because there cannot be an ordinary dismissal where the contract is not continuing. The woman will be taken as having been employed until the NDR and dismissed with effect from that date. She can use the deemed dismissal as the basis for ordinary claims for unfair dismissal and redundancy, and claims for automatically unfair dismissal and sex discrimination.

## Exceptions to deemed dismissals

There will not be a deemed dismissal under s 96(1) ERA where either:

- It is not reasonably practicable for a reason other than redundancy for the employer to allow the woman to return to work, and she has either accepted or unreasonably refused an offer of suitable alternative employment (s 96(3) ERA); or

- Where the employer and any associated employer employ a total of not more than 5 employees, and it is not reasonably practicable for any reason to allow the woman to return to work or to offer her suitable alternative employment (s 96(2) ERA). The total number of employees includes the woman herself and is taken immediately before the end of the first 14 weeks of leave (or if she is dismissed during the first 14 weeks, immediately before her dismissal).

### Example

Due to a business reorganisation, a woman with a statutory right to return from extended maternity leave is offered a different job to the one she did previously. She refuses and claims unfair dismissal. The tribunal decides that the alternative job was suitable and that the woman's refusal to accept it was unreasonable. As a result there is no deemed dismissal under s 96(1) ERA and the woman is not entitled to compensation for the loss of her job.

## Dismissals for redundancy

Employers frequently want to refuse the right to return to work from maternity leave on the grounds that the woman's job is "redundant". In many cases the job will not be redundant at all; rather the employer has engaged a replacement during the woman's absence on maternity leave, and would prefer to retain the replacement at the expense of the woman who has taken leave. This is clearly not a redundancy situation, and the employer's refusal to let the woman return to her old job will amount to unfair dismissal and sex discrimination *(Rees v Apollo Watch Repairs plc* [1996] ICR 466).

If there is a genuine redundancy situation, a woman who is pregnant or on maternity leave may be fairly dismissed for redundancy, provided the employer complies with the normal requirements of applying objective selection criteria and offering any suitable alternative work which is available. There are however some particular points to note in relation to these requirements.

## Selection criteria

If a woman is selected for redundancy because of one or more of the reasons set out in s 99 ERA, her dismissal will automatically be unfair by virtue of s 105 ERA. The s 99 ERA reasons are examined below. They include reasons connected with pregnancy, maternity leave and the special health and safety provisions relating to pregnancy and childbirth (see Chapter 18).

### Example

An employer has to choose between two female employees to decide whom to make redundant. He chooses the one who is about to take maternity leave so that he does not have to take on a replacement for her and provide her benefits during her leave. The woman is being selected on the grounds of her pregnancy and her wish to take maternity leave, and the dismissal for redundancy is automatically unfair under s 105 ERA. The woman can also claim sex discrimination.

## Offering suitable alternative employment

Where a woman is made redundant during her maternity leave, the employer must offer her any suitable vacancy (ss 77 and 81 ERA). Failure to do so will render her dismissal automatically unfair under s 99 ERA regardless of her length of service. The precise nature of this obligation depends on whether the woman is taking basic or extended maternity leave.

If the woman who is made redundant is on basic maternity leave, the employer must offer her a suitable alternative job if one is available at the time of her redundancy.

If the woman is taking extended maternity leave, the employer must offer her any suitable alternative job which is either available at the time of her redundancy or which becomes available at any time during the remainder of her leave. This applies regardless of whether the woman has given notice of her intended date of return under s 82(1) ERA before the vacancy arises (*Philip Hodges & Co* v *Kell* [1994] ICR 656).

---

**Example**

A woman's job becomes redundant half way through her extended maternity leave because her employer closes down the part of the business in which she worked. When the redundancy occurs there is no suitable work available elsewhere in the business. Four weeks later a suitable vacancy arises in the business but the employer does not offer it to the woman. As a result she can claim automatically unfair dismissal under s 99 ERA. It does not matter that the vacancy has arisen before she has given notice of her intended date of return.

---

Where the employer is making several people redundant, the effect of ss 77 and 81 ERA appears to be that any suitable vacancies must be offered to those women who are on maternity leave, even if those employees who have not taken leave are better qualified.

Where a suitable vacancy does exist, the employer cannot argue that it was not economic or reasonable to offer it to the woman on maternity leave (*Community Task Force* v *Rimmer* [1986] ICR 491). If a woman unreasonably refuses an offer of a suitable alternative job, her dismissal will be fair and she will not be entitled to a redundancy payment.

## Meaning of suitable alternative employment

The question of whether suitable alternative employment has been offered arises not only in relation to redundancy but also where the employer is claiming an exception to a deemed dismissal under s 96 ERA on grounds other than redundancy, *e.g.* where there is a business reorganisation.

A suitable alternative job is one in which:

- the work to be done is suitable in relation to the employee; and

- it is appropriate for her to do in the circumstances; and

- her terms and conditions (including terms relating to capacity and place of work) are not substantially less favourable than they would have been if she was still doing her old job (s 96(4) ERA).

The alternative employment may be with the original employer, his successor or an associated employer.

### Example

In *Hill* v *Supasnaps Ltd* COIT 1930/200 Ms Hill had been the branch manager of a shop. Whilst she was on maternity leave, the company changed hands. As a result the business was reorganised and changes were made to the branch managers' jobs. When Ms Hill came to return to work, she was told that there was no vacancy at her old branch, but that she could have a similar job at either of two other branches. Ms Hill refused and said that the offers were unsuitable because the jobs would involve extra travelling time and child care costs. The tribunal ruled that Ms Hill had been unfairly dismissed because her employer could not show that her old job no longer existed, and there was no provision in her contract which allowed the employer to change her place of work. The tribunal went on to say that, even if her job did no longer exist, the offers of alternative work were not suitable due to the extra travelling time and child care costs which they would have involved.

## Automatically unfair dismissals

In some circumstances, the dismissal of a woman who is pregnant or who takes maternity leave will be automatically unfair regardless of the length of her service with the employer. The circumstances are set out in s 90 ERA and include the following.

- Where the reason or principal reason for the dismissal is that the woman is pregnant, or any other reason connected with her pregnancy.

   This provision will be given a wide interpretation by industrial tribunals, and will include dismissals for pregnancy related illnesses (whether before or after childbirth) and where an employee is absent due to a miscarriage.

   The employer will not be liable under this provision unless he knew or believed that the woman was pregnant or, where the dismissal was for a reason connected with the pregnancy, he knew of the connection with pregnancy.

### Example

In *Nashanand* v *James Crowe (Cases) Ltd* COIT 881/57 a woman was dismissed for absenteeism. She had never told the company that she was pregnant, and it was only after the dismissal that the company discovered that she had had a miscarriage. The tribunal decided that the dismissal was fair.

- Where a woman is dismissed during her basic maternity leave period and the principal reason for the dismissal is that the woman has given birth or it is for any other reason connected with her having given birth.

- Where a woman is dismissed after her basic maternity leave period because she took maternity leave or made use of the benefits she was entitled to during her leave.

### Example

A woman is contractually entitled to private use of a company telephone. She takes basic maternity leave and uses the telephone during her leave in accordance with her contract. On her return to work the company dismisses her for having used the telephone. The dismissal will automatically be unfair.

- Where, before the end of her basic maternity leave, a woman gives her employer a medical certificate stating that she will be incapable of work after the end of that period by reason of disease or bodily or mental disablement, and she is dismissed within 4 weeks following the end of her basic maternity leave period in circumstances where she continues to be incapable of work and the medical certificate remains current, and the principle reason for the dismissal is that she has given birth or any other reason connected with her having given birth.

- Where an employer dismisses a woman to avoid having to suspend her from work on health and safety grounds because of pregnancy, recent childbirth or the fact that she is breastfeeding (see Chapter 18).

- Where the woman's job becomes redundant during her maternity leave and the employer fails to offer her a suitable alternative vacancy (see above).

## Written reasons for dismissal

If an employee is dismissed whilst she is pregnant, or if she is dismissed after childbirth and her basic maternity leave period ends by reason of the dismissal, she is entitled to receive from her employer written reasons for the dismissal regardless of her length of service and whether or not she has requested them from her employer (s 92(4) ERA).

## Maternity leave replacements

Employers will often need to recruit temporary replacements for employees who are taking maternity leave or who are suspended from work for health and safety reasons (see Chapter 18).

In some circumstances, the replacement employee may have accrued sufficient continuous service to pursue a claim for unfair dismissal if she is dismissed when the original employee returns to work.

Where this is the case, the employer may be able to rely on s 106 ERA to establish a fair reason for the dismissal. The employer has to show that:

- the employer informed the replacement in writing at the time of engagement that his or her employment will be terminated on the resumption of work by another employer who is, or will be, absent wholly or partly because of pregnancy or childbirth; and

- the dismissal occurs so that work can be given to the returning employee (s 106(2) ERA).

Similar provision is made by s 106(3) ERA in respect of replacements for employees who have been suspended from work on health and safety grounds because of pregnancy, recent childbirth or the fact that they are breast-feeding.

Whilst prudent employers will follow the requirements of s 106 ERA on engaging temporary replacements, a failure to give the written notice does not mean that the eventual dismissal of the replacement will be automatically unfair. The employer may still be able to show that there was a fair reason for the dismissal under s 98 ERA.

If the original employee decides not to return to work, the temporary replacement does not have an automatic right to the position on a permanent basis. If the job is given to someone else, and the replacement claims unfair dismissal, the employer may be able to show that the replacement was unsuitable for a permanent position and that the dismissal is fair for "some other substantial reason" under s 98(1) ERA.

Difficulties may occur if a temporary replacement becomes pregnant during her employment. If she is dismissed because of her pregnancy, the dismissal will be automatically unfair under s 99 ERA, and it may amount to sex discrimination (see below).

If the employer decides that the temporary replacement is more suited to the job than the employee who is taking maternity leave, the employee on leave must nevertheless be allowed to return to her old job. A refusal by the employer will amount to unfair dismissal and sex discrimination (*Rees* v *Apollo Watch Repairs plc* [1996] ICR 466).

## Sex discrimination and pregnancy

### General principle

Any less favourable treatment of a woman because of her pregnancy or the consequences of her pregnancy amounts to direct sex discrimination (*Webb* v *EMO Air Cargo (UK) Ltd* (No 2) [1995] ICR 1021).

### Example

A pregnant woman is dismissed because her employer says that he cannot afford to engage a temporary replacement during her absence on maternity leave. The dismissal is direct sex discrimination.

Unlike other instances of sex discrimination, no comparison is made between the treatment of a pregnant worker and a man in similar circumstances. Therefore, in the above example, the employer cannot argue that a man who was to be absent for the same period due to sickness would also be dismissed.

In determining whether the treatment of the woman is on the grounds of her pregnancy, it is only necessary for there to be a casual link between the pregnancy and the employer's actions. As in all cases of direct sex discrimination, the employer's motives behind the treatment are irrelevant.

### Example

In *O'Neill* v *Governors of St Thomas More Roman Catholic Voluntary Aided Upper School* [1996] IRLR 372 Mrs O'Neill was a teacher of religious education at the school. She had a relationship with a Roman Catholic priest and became pregnant. When this was discovered by the school's governors, they stopped paying her salary and told the local and national press what had happened. Mrs O'Neill resigned and claimed unfair constructive dismissal (see Chapter 29), and this was admitted by the governors. She also claimed sex discrimination on the basis that the constructive dismissal was on the grounds of her sex. The industrial tribunal found that there was no sex discrimination, ruling that Mrs O'Neill had been dismissed not because of the pregnancy per se, but because the pregnancy was by a Roman Catholic priest, which made her position at the school untenable. Mrs O'Neill appealed to the EAT, who ruled that the tribunal's approach was incorrect, and that the reasons behind her treatment were all related to the fact that she was pregnant. In view of this, Mrs O'Neill had been treated less favourably on the grounds of her sex, which amounted to direct sex discrimination.

## Fixed-term contracts

In the *Webb* v *EMO* case (above) Mrs Webb had been engaged to replace a woman who was on maternity leave, and then became pregnant herself. As a result the company dismissed her, and this was ruled by the House of Lords (having referred the case to the ECJ) to be sex discrimination.

Although Mrs Webb was initially engaged as a maternity replacement, she was employed under an indefinite contract rather than a fixed-term one. When the ECJ considered the case, it emphasised the indefinite duration of Mrs Webb's contract. The House of Lords noted this, and thought that this emphasis suggested the possibility of a distinction between such a case and the case where a woman's absence due to pregnancy would have the consequence of her being unavailable for the whole of the work for which she had been engaged. In the House of Lords' view, if it were not possible to distinguish these two situations, the result could be regarded as unfair to employers and likely to bring the law on sex discrimination into disrepute. However the House of Lords did not actually decide that Mrs Webb's dismissal would not have been discriminatory if her contract had been for a fixed term.

The point was considered further in *Caruana* v *Manchester Airport plc* [1996] IRLR 378. Mrs Caruana had been employed under two consecutive fixed-term contracts, the second of which was due to expire on 31 December 1992. On 16 November 1992 she notified the company that she was going on maternity leave on 11 December 1992, and that she intended to return to work after her leave. However on 3 December 1992, she was told that her contract would not be renewed.

The EAT ruled that, although the company had decided not to offer Mrs Caruana a new contract because of her unavailability for work, her unavailability was due to her pregnancy, and therefore the company's actions amounted to direct sex discrimination.

The EAT said that Mrs Caruana's complaint concerned the company's failure to extend her employment. In the EAT's view, this was a long way from the situation identified by the House of Lords in *Webb* v *EMO* as being a possible exception to the general principle, that is, where the employee would be unable to perform any part of a one-off contract.

The EAT also thought that, if Mrs Caruana's claim came within an exception to the general principle, it would encourage employers to offer or impose a series of short-term contracts, rather than a continuous and stable employment relationship, with the object of avoiding the discrimination laws. The EAT was sure that the ECJ and the House of Lords could not have intended this to be the case.

The EAT did not consider whether the possible exception put forward by the House of Lords in *Webb* v *EMO* is part of the law. It therefore remains possible that the dismissal of a woman employed on a one-off fixed-term contract (*e.g.* maternity replacements or, as suggested by the House of Lords, workers at events such as Wimbledon or the Olympic

Games) because her pregnancy will make her unavailable for the remainder of her contract, will not be sex discrimination. No doubt the point will be determined in the near future.

## Dismissals during pregnancy on non-pregnancy grounds

> **Example**
>
> In *Quaynor* v *Optika Ltd* COIT 25564/95 a woman was dismissed for redundancy just before her maternity leave was due to begin. The industrial tribunal accepted that there was a genuine redundancy situation and that her dismissal was entirely unconnected with her pregnancy. However the tribunal went on to find that the dismissal was sex discrimination on the basis that a pregnant woman should not be dismissed for any reason until her maternity leave period has ended. The tribunal justified its decision on the basis that the dismissal of a pregnant woman may have an adverse effect on her mental or physical state. This principle was derived from the EC Pregnant Workers' Directive (No 92/85) which provides that a pregnant woman should not be dismissed "save in exceptional circumstances not connected with her condition which are permitted under national legislation and/or practice".

The tribunal's decision is somewhat unusual, and its line of reasoning does not appear to have been applied in any other case concerning the dismissal of a pregnant woman.

## Pregnancy-related illnesses and the "protected period"

In addition to a claim under s 99 ERA for automatically unfair dismissal, a woman who is dismissed due to a pregnancy-related illness may have a claim for sex discrimination.

In *Handels-Og Kontorfunktionaerernes Forbund i Danmark (acting for Hertz)* v *Dansk Arbejdsgiverforening (acting for Aldi Marked K/S)*

[1992] ICR 332 (known as the *Hertz* case) the ECJ established the idea of a "protected period", which runs from the onset of pregnancy until the end of the woman's statutory maternity leave. If the woman is dismissed for a pregnancy-related illness during the protected period, this will amount to sex discrimination.

If a woman is dismissed following her return to work due to a pregnancy-related illness, the dismissal will be outside the protected period and a comparison can be made with the treatment of a sick man to determine whether the dismissal amounts to sex discrimination. If the employer can show that a man would have been dismissed after a similar period of sick leave, the woman's claim for sex discrimination will probably fail. However in making the comparison between the man and the woman, the woman's absence during the protected period should be disregarded.

The "protected period" may also be relevant where dismissals occur following pregnancy for reasons not connected with illness. In *British Telecommunications plc* v *Roberts* (EAT 315/95) two employees claimed sex discrimination when their request to job-share on returning from maternity leave was refused. The tribunal decided that this amounted to direct sex discrimination following the decision in *Webb* v *EMO* (above), because their treatment followed directly from their pregnancies. However the EAT ruled that the specific protection provided to women in connection with pregnancy does not extend beyond the protected period, which ends when a woman returns to work from statutory maternity leave. Because the employer's refusal was concerned with the arrangements being made after the employees had returned to work, it did not amount to direct sex discrimination. The EAT remitted the case to the tribunal to determine whether the refusal constituted indirect sex discrimination (see above).

## Paternity leave

There is no statutory right under UK law to paternity leave and, because s 2(2) SDA expressly provides that the special rights given to women in connection with pregnancy and child birth are not discriminatory, men cannot claim an equivalent right under the SDA.

In March 1996, the EU Social Affairs Council adopted the Parental Leave Directive, which allows workers of both sexes to take unpaid parental leave of up to 3 months following the birth or adoption of a child. The Directive cannot be relied on by employees in the UK due to the opt-out negotiated by the government at Maastricht in 1991.

Although there is no obligation to provide paternity leave, many employers do allow fathers to take a limited period of paid or unpaid leave around the time of the birth in addition to their usual holiday entitlement.

## Summary
## Maternity and Paternity Rights

Maternity rights include: time off with pay for antenatal care; statutory maternity leave; the right to return to work after maternity leave; and unfair dismissal rights.

*Antenatal care*

- All employees regardless of length of service have the right to paid time off for antenatal care.

*Maternity leave*

- Women with less than 2 years' service are entitled to 14 weeks' maternity leave (basic maternity leave). Women with at least 2 years' continuous service are entitled to maternity leave for up to 40 weeks (extended maternity leave). Extended maternity leave may commence up to 11 weeks before the expected week of childbirth (EWC) and an employee will have the right to return to work up to 29 weeks after the week in which child birth occurs.

- In order to take basic maternity leave or extended maternity leave an employee must comply with certain notice provisions. A failure by the employee to comply with these provisions will cause her to lose her right to maternity leave.

- Employees will be entitled to various types of benefits under their contracts of employment during maternity leave. Different rules apply for basic maternity leave and extended maternity leave.

- With regard to continuity of service, different rules apply during basic maternity leave and extended maternity leave.

*Returning from maternity leave*

- Different rules apply for basic maternity leave and extended maternity leave.

- Women have a special right not to be unfairly dismissed for a pregnancy or maternity leave related reasons. In certain circumstances women with less than 2 years' service can claim automatically unfair dismissal.

- Employees have a right to return to their old job (or a comparable job), on terms and conditions not less favourable than those which would have applied to her if she had not been absent from work.

- Employers must consider all requests by women to return to work part-time. Failure to do so could give rise to a claim for indirect sex discrimination.

- Special rights apply to redundancies involving pregnant workers and workers on maternity leave including a right to be offered suitable alternative employment.

- Regardless of her length of service, if a woman is dismissed whilst pregnant or on maternity leave she is entitled to receive from her employer written reasons for the dismissal.

*Sex discrimination*

- Any less favourable treatment of a woman because of her pregnancy or the consequences of her pregnancy amounts to direct sex discrimination. Compensation is unlimited for sex discrimination.

*Paternity leave*

- Employees have no statutory right to paternity leave, although many employees now have contractual paternity rights.

# CONTENTS OF CHAPTER 20

## Hours of Work

# 20. HOURS OF WORK

This chapter looks at the potential for employers to discriminate in the allocation of working hours, shifts and sensible working arrangements, overtime and job sharing

## Race discrimination

The CRE Code of Practice points out that many employees from particular ethnic or racial groups will have particular cultural and religious needs. Employers should aim to be flexible in order to allow employees to observe prayer times, religious festivals and religious holidays (see Chapter 25).

## Sex discrimination

### Statutory rights

Until 1995, many part-time employees were denied certain statutory rights enjoyed by their full-time colleagues. This was due to Schedule 13 of the Employment Protection (Consolidation) Act 1978, which set out different qualifying thresholds for full-time and part-time workers. As a consequence, whilst an employee who worked at least 16 hours each week could claim a redundancy payment or unfair dismissal after 2 years' continuous service with his or her employer, those working between 8 and 16 hours had to have 5 years' service for such claims, and employees who worked less than 8 hours per week could not pursue such claims at all.

In *R* v *Secretary of State for Employment, ex parte Equal Opportunities Commission* [1994] ICR 317 the House of Lords ruled that the provisions relating to the rights of part-time workers to claim a redundancy payment indirectly discriminated against women, on the basis that a considerably greater proportion of women than men work part-time.

As a result of the House of Lords' decision, the Employment Protection (Part-Time Employees) Regulations 1995 (SI 1995/31) were introduced, which removed the distinctions based on hours worked each week in determining an employee's statutory rights.

This means that all employees can now claim, *e.g.* unfair dismissal and redundancy payments after 2 years' continuous service, regardless of the hours which they work each week.

## Flexible working

A far greater proportion of women than men have responsibility for looking after families. Employers need to ensure that any requirements they have concerning their employees' hours of work do not effectively prevent working mothers from doing the job, unless the requirements can be justified on grounds other than sex. Failure to do so may amount to indirect sex discrimination.

Employers are now encouraged to consider flexible working including offering career breaks to help women meet domestic responsibilities and pursue their occupations.

To minimise the risk of discrimination employers should consider, where possible, offering:

- part-time work;

- job sharing, (so that two people share one job, either working part of the day each, or part of the week each, or, alternate weeks depending on the employers needs and those of the employee);

- term-time working which would allow employees to work only during school term-time and not during the holidays;

- working from home;

- flexible working hours.

### Example

In *The Home Office* v *Holmes* [1984] ICR 678 a full-time employee with two young children applied to work part time. The Home Office refused because it had a general policy that part-time working would not be allowed at the employee's grade. The EAT ruled that the refusal was indirect sex discrimination. The proportion of women who could comply with the requirement to work full-time was considerably smaller than the proportion of men who could comply because of women's family commitments, and the requirement could not be justified in this case.

For a further discussion of flexible working, see Chapter 19.

## Disability discrimination

Employers should be prepared to make reasonable adjustments to accommodate disabled workers including by making alterations to working hours (see Chapter 3).

### Example

An employer could allow a disabled employee to "bank" any overtime hours worked (rather than be paid for the overtime), and those hours could be "redeemed" by the employee to compensate for any periods when the employee was unable to attend work during normal working hours because of their disability.

# CONTENTS OF CHAPTER 21

*Language*

# 21.  LANGUAGE

## Race discrimination

Many jobs require a knowledge and command of written or spoken English. For example, a switchboard operator who could not speak English or a typist who could not write in English would be of little value to an employer. However, many manual jobs do not require the job holder to speak or write English to a high standard (or at all). As discussed in Chapter 7, a requirement that applicants for such jobs should pass an English test could amount to indirect race discrimination against ethnic minority workers.

The CRE Code of Practice recommends that employers should not require a standard of English higher than that needed for the safe and effective performance of the job and should not disqualify applicants who are unable to complete an application form unassisted, unless personal completion of the form is a valid test of the standard of English required for the safe and effective performance of the job.

## Language training

The CRE Code of Practice states that, whilst there is no legal requirement to provide language training, difficulties in communication can endanger equal opportunities in the work force. The CRE recommend that where the workforce includes employees whose English is limited, employers should take steps to ensure the communications are as effective as possible. Employers should where reasonably practical provide:

- interpretation and translation facilities, *e.g.* in the communication of grievance and other procedures, and the terms of employment;

- training in English language and communications;

- training for managers and supervisors on the background and culture of racial minority groups;

- alternative or additional methods of communication, where employees find it difficult to understand Health and Safety requirements, *e.g.*

  – safety signs;
  – translation of safety notices;

–      instructions through interpreters;
–      instruction combined with industrial language training.

As mentioned in Chapter 9, employers can take some positive action to promote equality of opportunity without falling foul of the anti-discrimination law. In the case of language training, this can be provided by employers to meet special needs of ethnic minority employees. However, language training should not just be limited to ethnic minority employees, but could be offered (wherever possible) to all employees who will benefit from language training.

# CONTENTS OF
# CHAPTER 22

*Employee Mobility and Changing the Place of Work*

# 22. EMPLOYEE MOBILITY AND CHANGING THE PLACE OF WORK

## Introduction

An employee is entitled to be employed at the place of work specified in his or her contract of employment. Unless the contract also contains a mobility clause (either expressly or impliedly), any change by the employer in that place of work will be a breach of contract, even if the distance between the old and new places of work is small. There are many reasons why an employer will want to change the place of work, and it is therefore sensible to include clearly drafted mobility clauses in contracts of employment.

## Mobility must not be related to sex

Employers must however ensure that their mobility requirements do not amount to indirect sex discrimination by adversely affecting a much higher proportion of women than men (Chapter 2).

### Examples

In 1985 the EOC carried out a formal investigation of the Leeds Permanent Building Society. The Society had a requirement that all staff above a certain grade must be willing to be mobile across the country. This was found to be indirectly discriminatory against women because a much smaller proportion of women than men could comply with the requirement. In view of the EOC's investigation the Society adopted a new policy on mobility so that women were just as able as men to comply.

The Court of Appeal looked at the discriminatory effect of a mobility requirement, and the justification for it, in *Meade-Hill* v *The British Council* [1995] ICR 847. Mrs Meade-Hill was promoted and was required to accept a new contractual term that she should serve wherever in the UK her employer might direct. As a married woman earning less than her husband, she would have found it difficult to move her place of work if required to do so. At the time of Mrs Meade-Hill's promotion, her employer was considering moving a number of employees from London to Manchester, but in the event Mrs Meade-Hill was not required to move and the mobility clause was not invoked against her.

The Court of Appeal ruled that the mobility clause in Mrs Meade-Hill's contract of employment would give rise to indirect sex discrimination, unless her employer could show that it was justifiable on grounds unrelated to sex. The court accepted that a higher proportion of women than men are secondary earners, and consequently the proportion of women who could comply with a change of workplace which involves a change of home was considerably smaller than the proportion of men who could comply. It did not matter that Mrs Meade-Hill had agreed to the clause, nor that her employer had not actually invoked it.

The Court of Appeal pointed out that its decision did not mean that Mrs Meade-Hill had won a "great and glorious victory". All the employer had to show to justify the clause was a need to be in a position, if circumstances so required in the future, to direct an employee of her level to work elsewhere in the UK, even if that employee could not in practice comply with such a direction.

The court also said that, if the clause could not be justified in its existing form, it could be made lawful by modifying it, so that any employee of either sex who was unable to comply with the clause in practice could not be required to do so.

# CONTENTS OF CHAPTER 23

*Pension Benefits and Access to Pension Schemes*

# 23. PENSION BENEFITS AND ACCESS TO PENSION SCHEMES

There have been a number of cases exploring the exact scope of Article 119 of the Treaty of Rome 1957 (see Chapter 14) in relation to pensions and pension benefits. The ECJ has ruled that Article 119 implies equality of treatment for men and women in respect of pension benefits paid under a private occupational scheme where the scheme:

- supplements benefits payable under any relevant state pension scheme; or

- provides benefits which are, at least in part, a substitute for those provided by the state pension scheme.

Equality of treatment for men and women in relation to pension benefits may be claimed only in relation to benefits payable for periods of employment following 17 May 1990 (being the date of the judgment of the ECJ in *Barber* v *Guardian Royal Exchange Assurance Group* [1990] IRLR 240). This cut-off date was confirmed by the ECJ in *Ten Oever* v *Stichting* [1993] IRLR 601. Furthermore, an employee's dependants can rely on the equality obligation required in pension schemes and can enforce those obligations against the scheme trustees as well as the employer (*Coloroll Pension Trustees Ltd* v *Russell* [1994] IRLR 588).

Article 119 prohibits discriminatory conditions in the right of access to pay as well as discrimination in the quantum of pay. In *Barber* the ECJ decided that to apply an age condition, (which was different for each sex), to determine entitlement to benefits under an occupational pension scheme was contrary to Article 119.

## Part-time workers

In *Barber* the ECJ also decided that the exclusion of part-time employees from membership of an occupational pension scheme is unlawful. Two other ECJ decisions have had a significant effect on UK pension terms and equality. First, in *Vroege* v *NCIV Instituut Voor Volkshuisvesting BV* [1994] IRLR 651 the ECJ decided that Article 119 contained the right for part-time workers to demand to join an occupational scheme. Today, therefore, the exclusion of part-time staff must be justified by the employer by reference to factors unrelated to sex. If the exclusion of part-time workers from a pension scheme cannot be justified, then their exclusion will be contrary to Article 119. Furthermore a claim by a part-time worker to equal treatment in respect of membership of an occupational pension scheme could be backdated to 8 April 1976.

## Back-dated contributions

Secondly, the decision of the ECJ in *Fisscher* v *Voorhuis Hengelo BV* [1994] IRLR 662 confirmed that an employee's right to demand equal pension rights could be enforced against the scheme administrators as well as the employer. However, the ECJ also decided that any employee claiming pension scheme membership retrospectively to 8 April 1976 has to pay the employee's contributions relating to membership of the pension scheme for the relevant period.

### Disability and pensions

Employers must not discriminate in the provision of pension scheme benefits to disabled people, without justification.

**Summary**
**Pension Benefits and Access to Pension Schemes**

- Men and women are entitled to equality of treatment in respect of pension benefits paid under an occupational pension scheme for periods of employment following 17 May 1990.

- Part-time workers cannot be excluded from an occupational pension scheme and part-timers can bring claims for equal pension benefits back-dated to 8 April 1976. However, if they are successful they must pay the relevant employee's contributions to the scheme for the period during which they were entitled to be a member of the scheme but were excluded from it.

- Disabled workers cannot be excluded from pension schemes unless their exclusion can be objectively justified.

# CONTENTS OF CHAPTER 24

*Pressure to Discriminate*

# 24. PRESSURE TO DISCRIMINATE

Employers and employees who are accused of discrimination will be unable to hide behind an excuse that they were pressurised into committing an act of discrimination.

## Race and sex discrimination

Sections 30 and 31 RRA and 39 and 40 SDA make it unlawful to instruct or put pressure on others to discriminate on grounds of race or sex.

### Examples

An employer tells a Job Centre not to send any female candidates for interview. The employer's instruction is discriminatory.

A group of workers threaten to take industrial action if the employer recruits members of a particular racial group. The workers' threats are discriminatory.

An expression of preference is all that is needed to contravene the RRA and SDA. Threats or bribes are not necessary.

### Example

In *Commission for Racial Equality* v *The Imperial Society of Teachers of Dancing* [1983] IRLR 315 the ISTD wished to recruit someone of school-leaving age to carry out general clerical duties. The Secretary of the ISTD telephoned a local school and spoke to the Head of Careers. During the conversation, the Secretary said that she would rather the school did not send anyone coloured – because that person might feel out of place. The tribunal and EAT looked carefully at the meaning of the word "induce" in s 31 RRA and ruled that the Secretary's information did constitute an attempt to "induce" the school not to send coloured applicants for interview and was a discriminatory instruction.

## Motive

The motives of the person applying the pressure are irrelevant.

### Examples

Where a line manager is told not to recruit a woman, in the belief that only men will be able to cope with the existing all male environment in the work place, it is no defence to argue that the woman's best interests are at heart.

Similarly, an instruction to a Job Centre not to send any men for the post of secretary, on the basis that men will think that it is "women's work", is discriminatory.

It is not only employers and employees who can be liable for pressure to discriminate.

### Example

If a customer objects to an ethnic minority salesman on racial grounds and threatens to take his business elsewhere, he will have committed an act of discrimination.

An attempt to induce an act of discrimination will contravene the RRA and SDA, even if the person being put under pressure does not give way to it. Therefore if an employee, who is threatened with dismissal if he recruits a black assistant, recruits that assistant anyway, the threats will still amount to discrimination contrary to s 31 RRA.

The CRE Code of Practice makes the following recommendations:

- guidance should be given to all employees, and particularly those in positions of authority or influence, on the relevant provisions of the law;

- decision-makers should be instructed not to give way to pressure to discriminate;

- giving instructions or bringing pressure to discriminate should be treated as a disciplinary offence.

If an employer is being pressured to discriminate then the employer should consider taking disciplinary action against employees or reporting the pressuriser to the CRE or EOC as appropriate.

Only the CRE and EOC may institute proceedings where there has been pressure to discriminate. The proceedings are brought in the industrial tribunal, which can make a declaration that the act of discrimination complained of has taken place. The tribunal has no power to award a financial penalty. The CRE or EOC may apply for an injunction if, notwithstanding the tribunal's declaration, there is a further offence.

Although individuals cannot bring an action against the person or company applying the pressure, they can claim race or sex discrimination in the usual way if the pressure leads to an act of discrimination against them.

## Disability discrimination

There are no provisions in the DDA which are directly comparable to ss 30 and 31 RRA. However it is likely that an industrial tribunal will try to find that there has been discrimination where instructions have been given or pressure has been applied to commit a discriminatory act under the DDA.

# CONTENTS OF CHAPTER 25

*Religion*

# 25. RELIGION

## Race discrimination

Discrimination on religious grounds is not in itself unlawful, however, such discrimination is prohibited in Northern Ireland by the Fair Employment Northern Ireland Act 1976. England, Wales and Scotland do not have such legislation perhaps because religious discrimination is not considered to be widespread. However, religious discrimination can amount to indirect race discrimination. The law relating to specific religious groups is discussed below.

### Sikhs

The question of whether Sikhs are an ethnic group who are covered by the RRA has been considered by the House of Lords in *Mandla (Sewa Singh)* v *Dowell Lee* [1983] IRLR 209. The House of Lords ruled that Sikhs were a racial group and should be protected by s 3(1) RRA. Lord Fraser of Tullybelton set out requirements for a group to constitute an ethnic group under the RRA. He said:

"For a group to constitute an ethnic group for the purpose of the RRA, it must regard itself, and be regarded by others, as a distinct community by virtue of certain characteristics. It is essential that there is:

(1)     a long shared history, of which the group is conscious as distinguishing it from other groups, and the memory of which keeps it alive;

(2)     a cultural tradition of its own, including family and social customs and manners, often but not necessarily associated with religious observance;

(3)     either a common geographical origin, or descent from a small number of common ancestors;

(4)     a common language, not necessarily peculiar to the group;

(5)     a common literature, peculiar to the group;

(6)     a common religion different from that of neighbouring groups or from the general community surrounding it;

(7)     being a minority or being an oppressed or a dominant group
        within a larger community."

The House of Lords concluded that Sikhs are a group defined by reference to ethnic origins for the purpose of the RRA, although they are not
biologically distinguishable from other peoples living in the Punjab.

## Jews

Jews are not an ethnic group but are a religious group. However, if a
manager believes that Jews are a racial group and treats them
unfavourably because of that belief, then he is acting on racial grounds
whether or not his belief is correct and he will have committed an act of
discrimination.

## Muslims

See Chapter 12 for a discussion of discrimination against Muslims on the
grounds of race because of their dress codes.

## Gypsies

In *Commission for Racial Equality* v *Dutton* [1989] IRLR 8 the Court of
Appeal decided that gypsies were an identifiable group defined by reference to "ethnic origins" and could complain of race discrimination.

## Rastafarians

In *Dawkins* v *Department of the Environment* [1993] IRLR 284 the Court
of Appeal ruled that an industrial tribunal which upheld the complaint of
unlawful discrimination under the RRA had been wrong to regard
Rastafarians as a group defined by reference to "ethnic origins". There
was nothing to set Rastafarians apart as a separate ethnic group from the
rest of the Afro-Caribbean community. (Compare the discussion relating
to Sikhs, above.)

## Prayer times and religious holidays

Where employees have particular cultural and religious needs which compete with existing work requirements, employers should consider whether it is reasonably practicable to vary or adapt these requirements to enable such needs to be met. Examples of such needs include observance of prayer times and religious holidays. An employer's rule which prohibits workers from observing prayer times and religious holidays may give rise to successful claims for indirect race discrimination. Where possible employers should consider flexible working hours to accommodate religious observance, *e.g.* by allowing Jews to work on Sundays.

### Example

In *Hussain and Others* v *J H Walker Ltd* [1996] IRLR 11 Mr Hussain and other Muslims were employed as production workers. They complained that they had been indirectly discriminated against on grounds of race when they were disciplined for taking a day off work to celebrate Eid (one of the most important religious occasions in the Muslim calender) in breach of a new company rule that non-statutory holidays would no longer be permitted during the company's busiest months, namely May, June and July.

The company's Muslim employees, who made up about half of the production workers, had always been permitted to take a day off, either as part of their holiday entitlement or without pay. The new rule came into force in September 1991. On 8 June 1992 the company was informed that Eid would fall on 11 June. They decided that they were not prepared to vary the rule, even though the Muslim employees were willing to work additional hours in order to compensate for the day off.

The employees took the day off and when they returned to work, they were given a final written warning. The industrial tribunal found that whilst the company had acted for what it genuinely believed was a good business reason when it introduced the holiday rule, they nevertheless found that the rule was not justifiable, especially bearing in mind that the Muslims were willing to work additional hours to make up any backlog. The company had failed to satisfy the burden of proving that the requirement in question was not applied with "the intention of treating the claimant unfavourably on racial grounds". The company knew that Eid was important to Muslim employees and that they were the only employees affected by the application of the requirement or condition that no holiday should be taken within certain months. The fact that the company's reason or motive in adopting and applying the holiday policy was to promote its business, did not prevent the tribunal from inferring that the company wanted to produce a state of affairs in which the employees were in fact treated unfavourably on racial grounds.

The industrial tribunal awarded £1,000 to each of the employees. This sum was awarded for injury to feelings, the nature of the detriment suffered by the employees, their length of service, good work records, the upset and distress caused by the company's actions, the threatened consequences and the imposition of a final written warning by the company following the taking of the day off.

## Innocent motive

It should be noted that in *Hussain* the innocent motives of the company did not protect them from liability for race discrimination.

## Summary
## Religion

- Discrimination on religious grounds, whilst not in itself unlawful, may amount to indirect race discrimination.

- Employers should try to accommodate employee's demands for prayer times and religious holidays.

- The innocent motives of an employer in refusing religious holidays may not prevent the employer being liable for race discrimination.

# CONTENTS OF CHAPTER 26

## *Sexual Orientation and Transsexuals*

# 26. SEXUAL ORIENTATION AND TRANSSEXUALS

## Discrimination due to sexual orientation

### Position under UK law

There is no specific UK legislation outlawing discrimination on the grounds of sexual orientation. The SDA only covers discrimination due to a person's physical sex, not their sexual preferences. Therefore if, for example, an employer refuses to recruit a gay man or woman because of his or her sexual orientation, the employer's action is not in itself unlawful.

There are however some circumstances where the employer's actions may, nevertheless, amount to sex discrimination, giving the employee a claim under the SDA.

### Examples

An employer refuses to recruit a gay man when he would have recruited a gay woman. The man could show that he has been treated less favourably on the grounds of his sex and has therefore suffered direct sex discrimination.

In *Deacon* v *Grampian Regional Council* (EAT 629/94) the EAT assumed that an employer's refusal to employ anyone who has been charged with or convicted of a homosexual offence amounts to indirect sex discrimination. This is because certain male but not female homosexual activities are prohibited by law, and therefore the proportion of men who can comply with the employer's requirement may be considerably smaller than the number of women who can comply. In the event the point was not decided by the EAT as its decision was reached on other grounds.

## Harassment

Harassment of an employee due to his or her sexual orientation may,
however, amount to sex discrimination if the victim can show that a member
of the opposite sex would not have been treated in the same way.

## Position under European Community law

In *R* v *Secretary of State for Defence, ex parte Smith* [1996] IRLR 100 the
Court of Appeal reviewed the Ministry of Defence's ban on homosexuals
in the armed forces. It was claimed by the applicants, who had all been
dismissed from the armed forces due to their sexual orientation, that the
ban was contrary to the European Community's Equal Treatment
Directive, as the concept of sex within the Directive included not only a
person's physical sex but also their sexual orientation. The Court of
Appeal rejected this argument, saying that it could find nothing whatever
in the Directive or in the Treaty of Rome 1957, (the founding treaty of the
European Union), which suggested that they covered discrimination on
the grounds of sexual orientation.

The European Commission has however recommended that harassment due to sexual orientation be discouraged. The Court of Appeal in

*R* v *Secretary of State for Defence, ex parte Smith* (above) acknowledged this, but took the view that the European Community's Code of Practice on measures to combat sexual harassment (Chapter 16) is only concerned with unacceptable behaviour in the workplace and does not create rights in relation to discrimination due to sexual orientation.

The Court of Appeal's finding is in line with the views of the European Commission expressed in a written reply to an MEP given by its then president, Jacques Delors, on 29 November 1988. According to M Delors: "the Community has no powers to intervene in respect of possible discrimination by the Member States against sexual minorities. The powers deriving from the Treaty enable it to intervene only in the event of discrimination because of nationality and to ensure equal treatment of male and female workers in employment relationships . . ."

The position under European Community law may however be different following the decision of the ECJ in *P* v *S and Cornwall County Council*, a case concerning discrimination against a transsexual (see below).

The ECJ's approach in the *P* v *S* case may lead to a finding that discrimination on the grounds of sexual orientation comes within the Equal Treatment Directive, and the case of *Grant* v *South West Trains Ltd* COIT 1784/96 has been referred to the ECJ to determine the issue.

## Discrimination against transsexuals

Transsexuals are often wrongly confused with homosexuals. In simple terms, homosexuals are attracted to persons of the same sex, whereas transsexuals physically belong to one sex but feel convinced that they belong to the other sex.

### Position under UK law

As with sexual orientation, there is no UK legislation specifically outlawing discrimination against a person on the grounds that he or she is a transsexual. The SDA only deals with discrimination by reason of a person's physical sex, and does not cover less favourable treatment due to a person's transsexuality (*Ryder-Barratt* v *Alpha Training Ltd* COIT 43377/91). A transsexual will have the usual rights under the SDA if the actual reason for the discrimination is his or her physical sex.

**Example**

An employer dismisses a male transsexual for dressing as a woman, but admits that he would not have dismissed a female transsexual who came to work dressed as a man. The difference in treatment is due to the man's physical sex, not his transsexuality.

To establish discrimination on the grounds of sex under the SDA, a transsexual must compare his or her treatment with that of someone of the opposite physical sex as determined at birth.

**Example**

A male-to-female transsexual has a claim for sex discrimination under the SDA if she is treated less favourably than a female colleague on the grounds of sex, but not if she is treated less favourably than a male colleague. This is because she is still regarded as being a man for the purposes of the SDA.

## *Position under European Community law*

In *P v S and Cornwall County Council* [1996] IRLR 347 the ECJ ruled that the dismissal of a person on the grounds that he or she intends to undergo, or has undergone, gender reassignment, is discrimination on the grounds of sex contrary to the EC Equal Treatment Directive.

P was a manager in an educational establishment operated by Cornwall County Council. A year after being taken on by the Council, P informed S, the chief executive of the establishment, of his intention to undergo gender reassignment. This began with a period known as a "life test", during which P dressed and behaved as a woman, followed by surgery to give P the physical attributes of a woman. After undergoing minor surgical operations, P was given notice of dismissal.

P claimed sex discrimination against S and the Council, arguing that his dismissal amounted to less favourable treatment on the grounds of sex. The industrial tribunal found that the reason for the dismissal was the fact that P proposed to undergo gender reassignment. However the tribunal said that P's claim was not covered by the SDA, and that if P had been female before gender reassignment, the Council would still have dismissed her because of the operation. However the tribunal thought that P's treatment by the Council may be precluded by the Equal Treatment directive, and they referred the matter to the ECJ for a preliminary ruling.

In reaching its decision, the ECJ said that:

> "The scope of the Equal Treatment directive cannot be confined simply to discrimination based on the fact that a person is of one or other sex. In view of its purpose and the nature of the rights which it seeks to safeguard, the scope of the directive is also such as to apply to discrimination arising, as in this case, from the gender re-assignment of the person concerned."

The ECJ went on to say that such discrimination is based, essentially if not exclusively, on the sex of the person concerned. Therefore, where a person is dismissed on the ground that he or she intends to undergo, or has undergone, gender reassignment, he or she is treated unfavourably by comparison with persons of the sex to which he or she was deemed to belong before undergoing gender reassignment. In the ECJ's view, to tolerate such discrimination would be tantamount to a failure to respect the dignity and freedom to which the person is entitled, and which the court has a duty to safeguard.

As a result of the ECJ's decision, European Community law does not allow employers to argue that the dismissal of a male-to-female trans-sexual will not be sex discrimination if a female-to-male transsexual would also have been dismissed, and vice versa. Furthermore, a male-to-female transsexual who is treated less favourably than her male col-leagues (*e.g.* because the employer gives an ex gratia bonus to all men but not women) can claim sex discrimination under European Community law, because under European Community law her treatment is compared with that of someone of the sex to which she belonged prior to her gender reassignment. Under UK law, she would still be regarded as a man and her treatment would be compared with that of her female colleagues.

## Unfair dismissal claims

The law relating to unfair dismissal generally is outside the scope of this book. However, employers should note that, even if their discriminatory actions towards gay men and women and transsexuals do not constitute unlawful sex discrimination, they may give rise to claims by employees for unfair dismissal.

---

**Example**

An engineering company adopts a policy of dismissing all employees who are gay, regardless of their sex. There is no unlawful discrimination, but the employees concerned are likely to have good claims for unfair dismissal, subject to meeting the usual requirements for unfair dismissal claims.

---

# CONTENTS OF CHAPTER 27

## Statutory Offices and Statutory Requirements

# 27.   STATUTORY OFFICES AND STATUTORY REQUIREMENTS

## Statutory offices

Although civil servants can present complaints under the discrimination laws, there is one class of crown servants whose special status denies them that right. These are the holders of "statutory offices". A statutory office is one created in pursuance of a statute. The holders of a statutory office include:

- ministers of the Crown;
- judges and Justices of the Peace;
- The Commissioners appointed to the CRE and EOC.

Such persons cannot bring any claim under the RRA, SDA or DDA. However, where persons are being appointed to such offices, the minister of the Crown or government department appointing them must not discriminate against them either in making the appointment or in the selection process. If a minister or department did discriminate, then the aggrieved person would have no remedy personally but the EOC or CRE as appropriate could take action.

## Police officers

Whilst the office of police constable is a statutory office, a police officer or a person applying to join the police force has the same rights as any other employee or job applicant under the RRA, SDA or DDA. There are special provisions under which regulations may permit a limited amount of discrimination in relation to both police and prison officers. Men and women may be treated differently in requirements relating to height, uniform or equipment, or allowances in lieu of uniform or equipment. Accordingly, a man wishing to join the police or prison service cannot complain under the SDA on the grounds that the minimum height requirement for men is greater than that for women.

## Statutory discrimination and race discrimination

An act of racial discrimination is lawful if it is done:

- in pursuance of any Act or Order in Council;

- in pursuance of any statutory rule or regulation;

- in order to comply with any condition or requirement imposed by a minister by virtue of any Act (s 41 RRA).

The statutory exception has been given a narrow interpretation by the courts. In *Hanson* v *Department of Education and Science* [1990] IRLR 302 a woman who was born in Hong Kong was qualified to teach there, but she was required by the Department of Education to take an extra qualification in order to teach in the UK. The Department argued that their requirement was authorised by statutory regulations. This defence was rejected by the House of Lords. The department would have had a defence only if the regulations had *required* them to act in the way they did. It was not sufficient that the regulations purported to authorise them to act in this way.

### *National security*

Section 42 RRA provides that race discrimination is not unlawful if it done for the purpose of safeguarding national security. A certificate to that effect by a minister is conclusive under s 69(2) RRA.

### *The armed forces*

The RRA provides that race discrimination is lawful in recruitment to the armed forces, if it is in accordance with the appropriate regulation. It is only on grounds of nationality or national origins that the regulations permit any discrimination. If a recruit is turned away on other racial grounds (*e.g.* because of his or her colour), he or she may present a complaint in industrial tribunal. Once a person has become a serving member of the armed forces, any kind of racial discrimination is forbidden, but he or she cannot make a complaint to an industrial tribunal. Instead, the complaint must be made and dealt with in accordance with the provisions and redress of grievances contained in the Army Act or in the corresponding Acts for the air force and the navy.

**PART IV**
*Discrimination and the Transfer of Undertakings*

# CONTENTS OF CHAPTER 28

## Discrimination and the Transfer of Undertakings

# 28. DISCRIMINATION AND THE TRANSFER OF UNDERTAKINGS

This chapter deals with discrimination in the context of the sale of a business and/or the "contracting in" or "contracting out" of services under the Transfer of Undertakings (Protection of Employment) Regulations 1981 (TUPE) (as amended). Whole books have been written about TUPE and we seek here only to outline the effect of TUPE and the relationship between TUPE and claims for race, sex and disability discrimination.

## Origins and purpose of TUPE

TUPE was enacted by the UK government to implement the European Communities Acquired Rights Directive of 1977 (Council Directive No 77/187). The purpose and intention of both the Directive and TUPE is to ensure that the jobs and the people that work in a business or undertaking are protected when that business or undertaking is transferred from one employer to another.

### How is protection achieved?

Prior to the introduction of TUPE, the transfer of a business terminated an employee's contract of employment thereby entitling the employee to potentially claim damages for wrongful dismissal, a redundancy payment or compensation for unfair dismissal.

The effect of TUPE is that the transfer will not terminate the contract of employment with the result that the new employer steps into the shoes of the old employer as the new employer of the old employer's employees; and all rights and liabilities connected with the employees' contracts of employment are transferred wholesale to the new employer with the exception of rights under an occupational pension scheme.

---

### Example

In *Barbara Adams* v *Lancashire County Council and Another* [1996] IRLR 154 the EAT upheld the long established view that occupational pension scheme rights were not transferred when an undertaking is transferred save for any terms in the pension scheme which relate to invalidity or survivor's benefits such as redundancy. Any such terms will be transferred. Furthermore, if an employee has a contractual right to require the employer to contribute to the employee's personal pension arrangement then that right will be transferred under TUPE as will other contractual benefits to which the employee may be entitled.

## Unfair dismissal and TUPE

Employees with more than 2 years' continuous employment are protected against being dismissed as a result of a TUPE transfer by the right to claim unfair dismissal. The two-year requirement has come under general attack by the Court of Appeal in *R* v *Secretary of State for Employment, ex parte Seymour-Smith and Perez* [1995] IRLR 464. However, the government has reaffirmed the need for employees to have 2 years of employment to claim unfair dismissal under TUPE by an amendment contained in the Collective Redundancies and Transfers of Undertakings (Protection of Employment) (Amendment) Regulations 1995.

In effect, the business transfer should make no difference from the transferring employees' point of view as their employment will continue with the new employer as if they had always been employed by the new employer.

## What is a transfer of an undertaking?

In 1986 in *Spijkers* v *Gebroders Benedik Abattoir (No 2)* [1986] CMLR 296 the European Court of Justice ruled that a transfer of an undertaking does not occur simply because there is a disposal of assets. It is necessary to consider whether the business is disposed of as a going concern. This would be indicated, where the operation of the business of the old employer is continued or resumed in the same or similar form by the new employer following the transfer. In the *Spijkers* case, the European Court of Justice set out what is known as the "shopping list" of factors to be taken into account in determining whether TUPE applies. The shopping list includes:

- the type of undertaking: TUPE usually applies to the sale of an entire business and to the contracting out of functions which do not necessarily form part of the employer's core business (*e.g.* security; word-processing; and catering);

- whether tangible assets (*e.g.* "plant" and buildings) have been transferred;

- whether "goodwill" has been transferred;

- whether the majority of employees are transferred;

- whether customers and work-in progress are transferred;

- the degree of similarity between the activities carried on before and after the transfer.

In *Schmidt* v *Sparr-Und Leihkasseder* [1994] IRLR 302 the ECJ confirmed that even where the operation which is the subject of the transfer was ancillary to the main object of the old employer's business this did not in itself exclude that activity from the operation of the Directive on which TUPE is formulated. Furthermore, the number of employees engaged in the undertaking is irrelevant; the key question is whether the business retains its identity after the transfer.

### Example

In the *Schmidt* case Frau Schmidt was employed by a German savings bank as the only cleaner at one of its branches. She was dismissed in February 1992 when, following the refurbishment of the branch at which she worked, the bank decided to entrust the cleaning of the premises to a cleaning contractor. It was ruled that the activity of cleaning the bank carried out by Frau Schmidt was an undertaking capable of being transferred as the same floor space at the bank needed to be cleaned following the transfer as was cleaned by Frau Schmidt before the transfer.

## Discrimination and TUPE transfers

In *DJM International Ltd* v *Nicholas* [1996] IRLR 76 the EAT decided that liability in respect of an alleged act of sex discrimination by the old employer transferred to the new employer on the transfer of an undertaking notwithstanding that the act complained of related not to the contract under which the employee was employed at the date of transfer but to an earlier contract of employment. The crucial question so far as the EAT was concerned was whether the act complained of was in respect of a particular person employed by the old employer in the undertaking transferred. The EAT decided that at the date of the transfer there was an employment relationship between the employee and the old employer and that the employee and her claim were transferred to the new employer.

Employers should recognise that industrial tribunals are likely to find that liability for claims for sex, race and disability discrimination will be transferred to the purchaser of the business or undertaking under TUPE. This emphasises the need for the new employer to make full enquiries of the old employer of any potential claims prior to the transfer taking place. If the new employer wants to be indemnified by the old employer in respect of such claims then the new employer will need to negotiate an indemnity from the old employer or a reduction in the purchase price before the transfer of the undertaking takes place.

# PART V
*Discrimination on the Termination of Employment*

# CONTENTS OF CHAPTER 29

*Dismissal*

# 29.  DISMISSAL

## Introduction

This chapter looks at how the dismissal, (including redundancy), of an employee can be an act of discrimination giving rise to a liability for the dismissing employer. It will also consider the relationship between claims for discrimination under the RRA, SDA and DDA and the right to bring a claim for unfair dismissal under the ERA. See also Chapter 19 for a discussion of the redundant employee who is on maternity leave.

## Dismissal amounting to discrimination

Discriminating against an employee on the grounds of race, sex or disability by dismissing him or her is made unlawful by ss 4(2)(c) RRA, 6(2)(b) SDA and 4(2)(d) DDA.

There is no requirement that the employee should have 2 years' service before bringing a claim. However an employee who wants to bring a claim for unfair dismissal under the ERA or under TUPE (see Chapter 28) must have completed 2 years' service at the effective date of dismissal.

When bringing a claim for race, sex or disability discrimination, the aggrieved employee will claim that by being dismissed, he or she was treated differently by the employer than the employer would have treated employees from other races, employees of the opposite sex, or employees who are not disabled.

The golden rule is that employers should not allow themselves to be influenced by the employee's race, sex or disability when deciding to dismiss.

### Example

In *Coles and Sodah* v *Bookwise Extra Ltd* COIT 139 Coles and Sodah were two of four contract workers involved in certain incidents which led to management splitting them up. In a subsequent argument about how management had been informed of the incident another employee said to Sodah, "it shows what a dumb coon you are". Sodah submitted a complaint about this, but this last incident prompted management to dismiss all four employees. Sodah successfully claimed race discrimination on the ground that but for his colour the remark would not have been made, and the incident would not have arisen and he would not have been dismissed. The tribunal agreed that this was a case of unlawful discrimination.

## Redundancy selection

It is important for management to ensure that those selecting candidates for redundancy are fully aware that they must not select candidates on the grounds of race, sex or disability or because of their own prejudices.

The CRE Code of Practice recommends that redundancy criteria should be examined to ensure that they are not unlawfully discriminatory. Employers should be cautious about adopting a "last in, first out" policy. There is a danger that if lower grade posts which are occupied by ethnic minority workers are chosen for redundancy ahead of managerial posts, then an act of indirect race discrimination may occur.

The EOC Code of Practice recommends that redundancy criteria affecting mainly one sex should be checked so that provisions which cannot be justified on non-sex grounds can be removed. Therefore, redundancy policy which says that part-time workers will be selected for redundancy ahead of the full-timers is likely to be indirectly discriminatory to women.

## Constructive dismissal

A constructive dismissal occurs where an employee resigns because the employer has breached a fundamental term of the employee's contract of employment.

### Example

In *Milovanovic* v *Habden Dying & Finishing Co Ltd & Others* COIT 2998/248 Mr Milovanovic resigned after being subjected to

> hostile comments relating to his national origin. The tribunal
> found that not only did these comments amount to race discrim-
> ination but they also amounted to a fundamental breach of the
> implied term of mutual trust of confidence between the employer
> and Mr Milovanovic giving rise to a claim for unfair constructive
> dismissal as well as giving rise to a claim for race discrimination
> under the RRA.

## Appeals against dismissal

Sections 4(2) RRA, 6(2) SDA and 4(2) DDA only relate to actions
committed in relation to current employees, and there is no protection at
all for former employees who are discriminated against in some way by
their old employers. That was the conclusion of the EAT in *The Post
Office* v *Adekeye (No 2)* [1995] IRLR 297 where Ms Adekeye claimed
that her appeal against her dismissal was conducted in a racially prej-
udiced way. The EAT however said that her contract of employment had
come to an end when she was dismissed and that as she was no longer an
employee at the time of the appeal hearing she was not entitled to claim
race discrimination under s 4(2)(c) RRA.

Employers should be wary of relying on this decision as acts of race
discrimination by employers during the appeal process may enable an
industrial tribunal to infer that the original dismissal of the employee was
itself conducted in a discriminatory way.

Employers with large numbers of ethnic minority staff, or with any
staff with language problems, should consider ensuring the disciplinary
rules and health and safety instructions are available in translation.

If an employee cannot understand the charges that are being made
against him or her, then they may have claims under both the RRA and
the ERA if the employer does not make adequate provision to ensure that
an interpreter is available. If a colleague is unable to assist the employee
then the CRE can provide a list of interpreters.

# PART VI
*Remedies for Discrimination*

## Introduction

Part VI looks at the remedies available to individuals in cases of race, sex and disability discrimination as well as equal pay claims under EqPA (see Chapter 14). Part VI also examines the powers of the CRE and EOC to take action in respect of discriminatory practices.

This section is not intended to be a comprehensive guide to industrial tribunal procedure in discrimination cases as that is a subject in itself. Guidance on relevant procedures can be obtained from industrial tribunals, solicitors, citizens advice bureaux and the CRE, EOC, NDC and NIDC.

# CONTENTS OF CHAPTER 30

## *Complaints to an Industrial Tribunal by Individuals*

# 30. COMPLAINTS TO AN INDUSTRIAL TRIBUNAL BY INDIVIDUALS

Two different groups have the right to take action against a discriminator for unlawful discrimination. This chapter looks at the rights of individuals and Chapter 31 considers the rights of the EOC and CRE.

A complaint by any person (the complainant) that another person (the respondent) has committed an act of discrimination against the complainant in the employment field may be presented to an industrial tribunal using Form IT1 (ss 54(1) SDA, 63(1) RRA, 8(1) DDA and 2(1) EqPA).

Unlike in cases of unfair dismissal there is no two-year qualifying period of service required before this entitlement arises in cases of discrimination or under EqPA. Only industrial tribunals have jurisdiction to hear complaints of unlawful discrimination in the employment field. Proceedings may be brought against more than one person, *e.g.* the person who committed the act of discrimination, the discriminator's employer and anyone who assisted the discriminator.

## Time limits

The time limit for presenting complaints of sex, race and disability discrimination is 3 months beginning when the act complained of was committed (ss 68(1) RRA, 76(1) SDA, Schedule 3 paragraph 3(1) DDA).

The date on which the act was committed depends on whether it is a single or continuing act. If it is a single act, then the date on which the act occurred is the relevant date, *e.g.* the date of dismissal, the date of a rejection for promotion or the date of a failure to appoint. In the case of a continuing act of discrimination, *e.g.* the operation of a discriminatory rule, the act is treated as done at the end of the period from which the complainant complains.

### Example

In *Barclays Bank plc* v *Kapur* [1991] IRLR 136 a refusal to credit past service by employees in Africa, who were of Asian origin, as pensionable service for the purposes of the bank's pension scheme, was treated as an act of discrimination which continued for the duration of the contract of employment.

Conversely, in *Sougrin* v *Haringey Health Authority* [1992] IRLR 650 the Court of Appeal refused to treat the placing of the applicant, a black nurse, in a lower pay grade as a continuing act so as to prevent the normal time limit from operating.

## *Equal pay*

A claim under EqPA (see Chapter 14) has to be presented during the period of employment or within 6 months of the end of the employment.

## *Extension of time limits*

Industrial tribunals have a discretion to extend the time limits if they consider that it is "just and equitable" to do so "in all circumstances of the case" (ss 68(6) RRA, 76(5) SDA and Schedule 3 paragraph 3(2) DDA). When exercising their discretion tribunals are entitled to take into account all matters which they consider to be relevant.

## Help for complainants from CRE or EOC

Complainants and prospective complainants can apply to the CRE or EOC for assistance with their case under s 66 RRA in the case of the CRE, and under s 75 SDA in the case of EOC. The CRE and EOC have a discretion to assist, *e.g.* where cases raise questions of principle or in extremely complex cases. The CRE or EOC's assistance may include giving advice about the dispute or arranging advice and representation for the complainant by a solicitor or barrister.

The CRE or EOC's expenses in helping a complainant will be deducted from any costs or expenses awarded to a successful complainant.

## Disability discrimination

Neither the NDC nor NIDC have the same powers to assist complainants as the EOC or CRE (see Chapter 3).

## Procedure for bringing a complaint

In cases of discrimination the burden of proof is on the complainant, and it is therefore particularly important that the complainant obtains as much information as possible from the respondent.

> ### Example
>
> In the case of an unsuccessful job applicant, the complainant will need information about the qualifications, sex and/or marital status and/or race of the successful candidate and other applicants for the job.

There are a number of procedures which are available to complainants to help them obtain information from the respondent following the commencement of tribunal proceedings.

### *Requests for further and better particulars*

Any party to the proceedings can apply to the tribunal for an order that further and better particulars be given by another party. Where a complainant fails to comply with an order for further and better particulars, the complaint may be dismissed completely or in part. As regards a respondent who fails to comply with an order, part or all of his response to the complaint (known as the Notice of Appearance) may be struck out.

### *The "questionnaire" procedure*

Sections 65 RRA, 74 SDA and 56 DDA provide a procedure which assists complainants to obtain information from the respondent before industrial tribunal proceedings have started or as a means of obtaining "further and better particulars" after proceedings have started.

The purpose of this procedure is to assist persons who think they have been the victim of discrimination to decide whether to start tribunal proceedings and then if they do, to help them to put together and present their case in the most effective way. The procedure consists of using a questionnaire which must be in the form prescribed by RRA, SDA or

DDA. The complainant's questions and the respondent's replies may be used as evidence in tribunal proceedings.

Whilst a respondent cannot be forced to answer the questionnaire, a tribunal may draw an adverse inference if the respondent employer unreasonably fails to reply or gives an evasive or equivocal response to a questionnaire.

The Sex Discrimination (Questions and Replies) Order 1975 and the Race Relations (Questions and Replies) Order 1977 set out time limits for serving the questionnaire on the respondent and rules governing the way in which the questionnaires and replies may be served on the other side. Similar rules are anticipated under the DDA.

A complainant may send a questionnaire to the respondent at any time before lodging the IT1 or within 21 days if the IT1 has already been lodged. Questionnaires served after the 21 days will only be permitted with the tribunal's permission.

The CRE and EOC can provide guidance on the preparation of questionnaires.

## Discovery and inspection of documents

Once proceedings have started, discovery (that is disclosure) by one party to the other of documents which are relevant and necessary for fairly disposing of the case or for saving costs, may be given voluntarily or by an order of the tribunal. Thus a complainant alleging discrimination in selection might request discovery and inspection of documents from the respondent which will show how the decision to appoint a particular candidate was reached. These would include documents showing the sex/racial distribution of the workforce generally, in particular jobs, and amongst the successful and unsuccessful candidates; details of qualifications of the other candidates; and the assessments and criteria used in the selection process.

The discovery procedure relates only to existing documents. Non-compliance by a respondent with an order for discovery may lead to a tribunal either striking out all or part of the notice of appearance, or preventing the respondent from defending the case. As regards the complainant, non-compliance with an order may result in the dismissal of the complaint.

The three main grounds on which employers may object to orders for discovery are:

- confidentiality of documents;
- the administrative burden of producing the documents; and
- public interest immunity.

The public interest immunity objection to an order for discovery has been held to apply in a case against the police in relation to statements taken by the officers investigating the complaint (*Mankanjuola* v *Commissioner of Police of the Metropolis* [1992] 3 ALL ER 617). The principle of the immunity is that the public interest served in maintaining confidentiality outweighs the public interest in ordering disclosure and securing that all relevant material is before the tribunal. In the above case, reliance by the Commissioner on immunity prevented a police officer obtaining production of police complaints and disciplinary files for the purpose of tribunal proceedings even though the information in such files was relevant to the issues in question in the case.

If appropriate, tribunals will inspect the documents to decide whether disclosure is necessary for the fair disposal of the case. The tribunal should then consider whether the necessary information could be obtained by other, more cost efficient means. Special measures may be appropriate such as, covering up irrelevant parts of the documents, or, substituting anonymous references for specific names, or having the case heard in private.

## Public hearings

In common with almost all other kinds of legal hearings, tribunal hearings are held in public and there are usually no restrictions on who may attend. Usually they are open to the press and details of proceedings can be freely reported. In certain circumstances, hearings in private may be appropriate, *e.g.* where it is necessary to protect confidentiality of evidence.

## Restricted reporting orders

In cases involving allegations of sexual abuse or harassment a tribunal may of its own initiative or on the application of a party make a "restricted reporting order". Before making such an order the tribunal will hear argument from the parties on whether an order is appropriate. If an order is made it will specify a person who is not to be identified until the tribunal has published its decision. Where a restricted reporting order is in force, it will be notified on the list of cases held by the tribunal and a notice will be put on the door of the tribunal.

## Remedies for sex, race and disability discrimination

A successful complainant (for sex, race or disability discrimination) is entitled to be awarded one or more of the following remedies:

- a declaration of the parties' rights;

- an order for compensation to the complainant;

- a recommendation that the discriminator should take remedial action (ss 65(1) SDA, 56(1) RRA and 8(2) DDA).

The choice of remedy depends on what the tribunal considers to be "just and equitable". As regards remedies under EqPA see Chapter 14.

### Declarations

A declaration is "an order declaring the rights of the complainant and the respondent in relation to the act to which the complaint relates" (ss 65(1) SDA, 56(1) RRA and 8(2) DDA). This may be appropriate in cases where the complainant has suffered no financial loss or where a point of principle is thought to be established, *e.g.* a declaration may state that the complainant is entitled to certain training facilities.

### Compensation

The tribunal may award compensation for most types of discrimination although compensation cannot currently be awarded for unintentional indirect race discrimination (see below).

Prior to 22 November 1993 in the case of sex discrimination, and 3 July 1994 in the case of race discrimination, the maximum amount of compensation which could be awarded for sex and race discrimination was £11,000 and no interest could be awarded in respect of the period prior to the date of the award. However, in the case of *Marshall* v *Southampton and South West Hampshire Area Health Authority (No 2)*

[1993] IRLR 445 the ECJ ruled that the limit of £11,000 and the failure to provide for interest on damages from the date of discrimination were contrary to the Equal Treatment Directive. As a result, the Sex Discrimination and Equal Pay (Remedies) Regulations 1993, which came into force on 22 November 1993, removed the limit on compensation for sex discrimination and equal pay cases and made provision for interest to be included in such awards. The limit of £11,000 in respect of race discrimination was removed with effect from 3 July 1994.

There is no limit on the amount of compensation that may be awarded in disability discrimination cases.

As the law currently stands, no compensation is payable in respect of indirect racial discrimination where the employer can prove that the requirement or condition was not applied with the intention of treating the complainant unfavourably on the grounds of race. The burden of proving this rests with the employer.

The position used to be the same for unintentional indirect sex discrimination. However the failure to provide for compensation in such cases came under increasing attack especially since the European Court of Justice's decision in the *Marshall (No 2)* case (referred to above) and also in *Dekker* v *Stichting VJ-Centrum Plus* [1992] ICR 325 in which the ECJ noted that the "[Equal Treatment] Directive does not make the liability of the discriminator in any way dependent upon evidence of fault." The final onslaught came from Mr Justice Mummery in the EAT case of *MacMillan* v *Edinburgh Voluntary Organisations Council* [1995] IRLR 537 in which he noted that the provisions of the SDA dealing with compensation for unintentional indirect discrimination could not be construed to accord with the Equal Treatment Directive.

Accordingly, with effect from 25 March 1996, the Sex Discrimination and Equal Pay (Miscellaneous Amendments) Regulations 1996 were introduced, which removed from the SDA the rule that no compensation could be awarded for unintentional indirect discrimination, but leaving the position unaltered so far as unintentional indirect race discrimination was concerned.

## Calculation of compensation

In assessing compensation, an industrial tribunal conducts a two-stage process. First, it has a discretion to award compensation in circumstances where it considers it "just and equitable" to do so. In other words, it must see whether compensation is an appropriate remedy. If a tribunal deems that compensation should be awarded, then it should calculate the compensation "for foreseeable damage arising directly from [the] unlawful act of discrimination" (*Coleman* v *Sky Rail Oceanic Ltd* [1981] ICR 864).

Compensation can cover financial loss attributable to the discrimination (*e.g.* lost wages, loss of pension rights, loss of future wages, loss of opportunity) and damages for injury to feelings, humiliation and insult.

Complainants have a duty to "mitigate" their loss which means that a complainant must take reasonable steps to reduce the loss caused by the discrimination and the compensation awarded may be reduced if the complainant fails to do so.

In the case of the *Ministry of Defence* v *Cannock* [1994] ICR 918 the EAT gave guidelines for the appropriate amount of compensation to be awarded to ex-service women who had been discharged from the armed forces when they became pregnant. The Ministry of Defence accepted that their policy of discharge was unlawful. The EAT decided that compensation should be assessed so as to put the complainant into the position she would have been in but for the unlawful act of discrimination. The EAT stressed that tribunals should "keep a due sense of proportion" when assessing compensation and should not treat the complainant as equivalent to a person who has lost a career because of a disability.

## Injury to feelings

One head of damages which is of particular importance in discrimination cases is that of injury to feelings, because such an award can be made notwithstanding the fact that the complainant has suffered no monetary loss. It can therefore apply in both dismissal and non-dismissal situations, and where the employee is immediately re-engaged in alternative employment. It remains to be seen how significant a role "injury to feelings" will play in awards of compensation under the DDA.

The size of awards in respect of injury to feelings depends entirely upon the circumstances of each case. In brief, it is for the industrial tribunal to weigh the evidence and to form a view as to the level of distress and humiliation that the applicant has shown to have been caused to her by the acts of discrimination (*Orlando* v *Didcott Power Station Sports and Social Club* [1996] IRLR 262).

Whilst it is difficult to give any hard and fast rule as to the amount of compensation to be awarded in respect of injury to feelings, the EAT in Scotland in *Shariff* v *Strathclyde Regional Council* [1992] IRLR 259 decided in a case of race discrimination that £500 for injury to feelings is "at or near the minimum appropriate award". In *Deane* v *London Borough of Ealing* [1993] ICR 329 the EAT increased the tribunal's award of £500 for injury to feelings to £1,000.

One issue that the tribunals are currently facing is whether the award for injury to feelings should be increased given the removal of the upper limit on the amount of compensation payable.

### Example

The case of *Orlando* v *Didcott Power Station Sports and Social Club* (above) concerned an appeal to the EAT by the applicant supported by the EOC, on the basis that an award of £750 for injury to feelings was too low considering the removal of the upper limit. It was noted by the EAT during the course of the case that the median award for this head of damages had remained at £1,000 (this figure did not include the MOD cases) since the removal of the cap on the size of awards that can be made. The EAT decided that the tribunal had been perfectly entitled to award £750 for injury to feelings having regard to the circumstances of that particular case.

However, it should be noted that higher awards for injury to feelings of between £2,000–£3,000 are becoming more commonplace. It also tends to be the case that awards for injury to feelings in racial discrimination cases are higher than those concerning sex discrimination.

In the case of *Noone* v *North West Thames Regional Health Authority* [1988] IRLR 195 the industrial tribunal awarded £5,000 for injury to feelings in a race discrimination case although the Court of Appeal subsequently reduced the award to £3,000. The court accepted that the complainant suffered severe injury to her feelings as a result of not getting the job, although she had not claimed compensation for her actual loss.

## Aggravated damages

Aggravated damages may also be included in a compensatory award in cases where the respondent has behaved in a high-handed, insulting, or, oppressive manner in committing a discriminatory act. A tribunal can also take into account unsatisfactory answers to a questionnaire served on a respondent.

---

### Example

In *Pratt* v *Walsall Health Authority* COIT 1943/6 two senior employees were found to have been involved in an extremely bad case of racial discrimination, but denied ever knowing that the complainant was black. Their failure to acknowledge or address the problem led to aggravated damages being awarded.

---

## Exemplary damages

Exemplary damages, that is damages awarded to punish the discriminator rather than to compensate the victim, cannot be awarded.

## Recommendation

The third remedy available to a tribunal is a recommendation for the purposes of removing or reducing the adverse effect of a discriminatory action on the complainant. Action can only be recommended to remove the adverse effects on a victim.

---

### Example

In *Thompson* v *Professional Pool Players' Organisation* (unreported) a tribunal decided that Miss Thompson had suffered sex discrimination when her application for membership of the organisation was refused. The tribunal recommended that Miss Thompson be admitted as a member of the organisation within 3 months from the date of the hearing.

---

Failure to comply with a recommendation can result in an increase in the compensatory award, or, if no compensation has been awarded, then an award of compensation may be made.

## Appeals

An appeal from a decision of an industrial tribunal may be made to the EAT only on a point of law. The most common ground of appeal is "perversity" (that is that the decision was perverse). An appeal from the EAT is to the Court of Appeal and requires the permission of the EAT or the Court of Appeal before it can be made. Further appeals can be made to the House of Lords if the Court of Appeal or House of Lords allows.

# CONTENTS OF
# CHAPTER 31

*Enforcement by the Commissions*

# 31. ENFORCEMENT BY THE COMMISSIONS

## Disability

Neither the NDC nor NIDC have powers in relation to the enforcement of the provisions of the DDA. Therefore, the rest of this chapter refers only to the EOC and CRE.

## Race and sex discrimination

The second group of persons who have the right to take action against a discriminator are the EOC and the CRE set up by s 53 SDA and s 43 RRA respectively.

The duties of the EOC and CRE are quite similar. The EOC's duties are:

- to work towards the elimination of discrimination;

- to promote equality of opportunity;

- to keep under review the working of the SDA and EqPA.

The CRE's duties are to:

- work towards the elimination of discrimination;

- to promote equality of opportunity and good relations between persons of different racial groups;

- to keep under review the workings of the RRA.

The EOC and CRE have the following general powers:

- to undertake research and educational activities which appear necessary or expedient;

- to assist (financially or otherwise) research or educational activities undertaken by others;

- to issue codes of practice;

- as regards the CRE to give financial or other assistance to organisations involved in the promotion of equality of opportunity and good relations between persons of different racial groups.

The Commissions have other powers in relation to the enforcement of the SDA, EqPA and RRA. These include the following:

- to give assistance to individuals in bringing cases under the SDA, EqPA and RRA;

- to conduct formal investigations (ss 57 SDA and 48 RRA);

- to issue non-discrimination notices (ss 67 SDA and 58 RRA);

- to apply for a decision as to whether certain types of unlawful discrimination have occurred (ss 72(2) SDA and 63(2) RRA);

- to apply for injunctions in certain cases (ss 71 and 72 SDA, 62 and 63 RRA).

The above powers are considered in more detail below.

## Formal investigations

The Commissions may conduct general investigations and investigations into the activities of a particular person or organisation (ss 57(1) SDA, 48(1) RRA). There are strict procedural requirements in relation to investigations by the Commissions.

## A "named person" or "organisation investigation"

A "named person" or "organisation investigation", (*e.g.* into the activities of a particular company), cannot be commenced until the Commission has sufficient evidence to believe that an unlawful act of discrimination may have occurred.

When starting an investigation the EOC or CRE must draw up terms of reference and must then give notice of the holding of the investigation either generally or to the particular persons named. If the investigation is into the activities of a particular person the EOC or CRE must offer the individual the opportunity of making oral and/or written representations. This provides the individual with an opportunity to try to persuade the Commission not to proceed or to limit the scope of their terms of reference.

In order to conduct investigations the EOC and CRE have the power to serve notices requiring the production of written information and documents and the attendance of witnesses to give evidence about the matters set out in the notice.

## Recommendations

Following a formal investigation the EOC and CRE may make recommendations to a person (*e.g.* an employer) or to the relevant Secretary of State which are not binding. Recommendations could include suggestions for changes to an employer's policies. They must also prepare a report of their findings in respect of any formal investigations which they have conducted. Such reports must be published or made available for inspection.

## Non-discrimination notices

The Commissions may issue non-discrimination notices if during the course of an investigation they are satisfied that a person is committing or has committed one of the following types of unlawful discrimination:

- unlawful discriminatory acts;
- discriminatory practices;
- discriminatory advertisements;
- pressure to discriminate; or
- breaches of an equality clause (EqPA only (see Chapter 14)).

Before serving a non-discrimination notice which has to be in a prescribed form the Commissions must give the person concerned a preliminary warning of its intention to issue a notice and tell him or her why. They must also offer the person an opportunity of making written and/or oral representations within a minimum of 28 days and they must take account of any such representations before issuing the notice.

After these steps have been taken the Commissions may issue the non-discrimination notice which must be based on findings of fact and the

Commissions must be satisfied that one of the unlawful acts set out above has been committed.

There is a right of appeal against any notice or requirement contained in a non-discrimination notice which must be started no later than 6 weeks after service of such notice.

## Public register

The Commissions have the power to investigate compliance with a non-discrimination notice for a period of up to 5 years following the issue of the notice. All non-discrimination notices which have become final are recorded in a register which is open for inspection by the public and from which copies of notices can be made.

## Decisions on unlawful discrimination.

The Commissions may apply to an industrial tribunal for a decision that an unlawful discriminatory advertisement has been published or that instructions or pressures to discriminate have taken place (ss 72 SDA, 63 RRA). An application for a decision must be made within 6 months from the time the act was done.

## Preliminary action

The Commissions may take action in an industrial tribunal against an alleged discriminator as a preliminary to taking injunction proceedings. The proceedings consist of presenting a complaint to an industrial tribunal that the discriminator has committed an act of unlawful discrimination and the tribunal must make a finding to that effect if they consider the complaint well founded. They may also make a declaration and/or a recommendation as if the complaint had been presented by the victim if they consider it just and equitable to do so.

## Injunctions

In cases of persistent discrimination the Commissions may apply to a county court or High Court for an injunction to restrain a person from committing an unlawful discriminatory act, an act in breach of an equality clause under EqPA (see Chapter 14) or an unlawful discriminatory practice. The application must be made within 5 years of:

- a non-discrimination notice becoming final; or

- a finding by a court or an industrial tribunal that the respondent has committed an unlawful discriminatory act or an act in breach of a term modified or included by virtue of an equality clause.

The court must be satisfied that the application is well founded and, if it is, it can grant the injunction in the terms applied for in more limited terms.

The Commissions may also bring injunction proceedings in respect of unlawful advertisements and pressure to discriminate if it appears that an act has been committed and that further acts will be committed unless the person is restrained.

The Commissions can only take proceedings where there is a final finding by the industrial tribunal that the discriminator has done an unlawful act.

# Appendix 1

## Equal Opportunities Policy

### A Co Ltd

#### Purpose and scope

1    A Co Ltd's policy is to offer equal treatment and opportunities in all aspects of employment to men and women regardless of their sex, sexual orientation, colour, marital status or family circumstances, race, nationality, ethnic or national origins, religious beliefs, political opinions, disability or age.

2    All members of staff have personal responsibility for the application of this policy.

3    Procedures and criteria for recruitment, promotion, transfer and training are based on this policy, and judgements as to suitability are made on the basis of the relevant merits and abilities of the individual.

#### Discipline

4    The Company considers any breach of this policy by a member of staff to be misconduct and will take appropriate disciplinary action against any individual who breaches this policy in accordance with the published Disciplinary Procedures.

#### How to report breaches of this policy

5    Where a member of staff considers that he or she has been subject to discrimination which is in direct conflict with this policy, he or she should normally register a complaint for investigation and resolution with the Personnel Manager.

# Appendix 2

## Sexual and Racial Harassment Policy

## A Co Ltd

### Purpose and scope

1   This policy statement is being issued to inform all directors, managers and other members of staff as to what the Company considers to be sexual harassment and racial harassment and how the Company will handle matters involving sexual harassment and/or racial harassment.

2   A Co Ltd strongly disapproves of and will not tolerate sexual or racial harassment.

3   This policy applies to all A Co Ltd directors, managers and other members of staff.

4   The Company will make every effort to ensure that everyone is familiar with this policy and understands that the Company will investigate thoroughly and resolve appropriately any complaint of sexual and/or racial harassment received.

5   The Company recognises that gender will affect the behaviour of people to others in many situations including at work. This policy statement addresses only harassment, to the exclusion of any other sex-related conduct which may be disruptive to the business of the Company for one reason or another and therefore necessarily relevant to employment. In this sphere, except as regarding harassment, A Co Ltd has not in the past and does not now seek to lay down express rules. The policy is for a relaxed and not a sombre work environment, which is best achieved when people conduct themselves with courtesy and consideration for others.

6   As the workplace brings together over a long time people who might not otherwise associate with each other, it seems a matter of good sense, as well as good manners, to avoid any behaviour which could be looked on as sexual and/or racial harassment. If there is a risk of it being unwelcome, there is a risk of it being harassment.

7   The Company welcomes any comments or suggestions as to how this policy may be improved.

### What constitutes sexual harassment?

8   The Company considers sexual harassment to be any action directed by a person at another of the same or opposite gender, regardless of the perpetrator's motives, which a reasonable person would find to be sexual harassment, including:

(a)   unwelcome verbal or physical conduct of a sexual nature, in particular unwelcome sexual advances or requests for sexual favours;

(b)   unsolicited sexually derogatory words or gestures;

(c)   showing or circulating written, printed or electronically disseminated material of a sexual nature which others may find offensive;

(d)   any other conduct of a sexual nature which may interfere with an individual's work performance or create an intimidating, hostile or offensive working environment;

(e)   any attempt to penalise or punish a person for rejecting or objecting to the actions described above.

## What constitutes racial harassment?

9   The Company considers racial harassment to be any action directed by a person at another of the same or different race, regardless of the perpetrator's motives, which a reasonable person would find to be racial harassment, including:-

(a)   unwelcome verbal or physical conduct of a racial nature;

(b)   racially derogatory words or gestures;

(c)   showing or circulating written, printed or electronically disseminated material of a racial nature which others may find offensive;

(d)   any other conduct of a racial nature which may interfere with an individual's work performance or create an intimidating, hostile or offensive working environment;

(e)   any attempt to penalise or punish a person for rejecting or objecting to the actions described above.

## Discipline

10   The Company considers sexual harassment and racial harassment to be misconduct and will take against any individual who breaches this policy appropriate disciplinary action, which includes summary dismissal without warning, in accordance with the Company's Disciplinary Procedures. The Company considers abuse of a position of authority for the purposes of sexual harassment to be reprehensible.

## How to report breaches of this policy

11   Everyone has the right to report breaches of this policy.

12   Any action by a director, manager or other member of staff which may constitute sexual and/or racial harassment should be reported immediately to the Personnel Manager or [          ], the person with specific responsibility for dealing with matters involving sexual and/or racial harassment.

13   In the event that a complainant has a valid reason not to report such harassment to the Personnel Manager or the person with specific responsibilities for sexual and/or racial harassment, he or she should report the action to the Managing Director.

14   All complaints will be fully investigated on a confidential basis and appropriate action will be taken. The complainant has, at all times, the right of access to the Managing Director in accordance with the Company's grievance procedure.

15   No person will suffer any adverse employment consequences as a result of reporting a breach of this policy, unless such a report shall be found to be either wholly false and unfounded or false and vexatious.

## Commitment of A Co Ltd to preventing sexual harassment and racial harassment

16   A Co Ltd trusts that all its directors, managers and other members of staff will continue to act responsibly to maintain a happy and professional working environment, free of sexual harassment and racial harassment.

17   Further, the Company is committed to:

(a)  publicising this policy to its directors, managers and other members of staff; and

(b)  providing new members of staff with a copy of this policy statement upon the commencement of employment with the Company; and

(c)  maintaining effective procedures for the enforcement of this policy, including the reporting of breaches.

# Appendix 3

## Maternity Policy and Notification Letter

## A Co Ltd

### 1 Introduction

This document sets out the company's policy on maternity leave and maternity pay. If you have any questions concerning this policy or any other aspect of your maternity rights you should speak to the personnel department.

### 2 Ante-natal care

You are entitled to reasonable time off from work with pay to attend doctors', midwives' and other antenatal care appointments. These should be arranged, if possible, at the start or end of the working day. As much notice as possible of appointments should be given to your supervisor/manager and the personnel department, and you should produce your appointment card.

### 3 Maternity leave

There are two categories of maternity leave:
1  basic maternity leave of 14 weeks;
2  extended maternity leave of up to 40 weeks.

#### 3.1  Basic maternity leave

You are entitled to basic maternity leave irrespective of your length of service or hours worked each week. It is governed by the following terms and conditions:

3.1.1  Maternity leave can commence at any time after the start of the eleventh week before the expected week of childbirth.

3.1.2  Absence due to a pregnancy related illness after the start of the sixth week before the expected week of childbirth will automatically start your maternity leave period and you will not be permitted to return to work until your baby has been born.

3.1.3  The personnel department must be informed in writing at least 21 days in advance, or if this is not possible, as soon as you can, of:
(a)  the fact that you are pregnant;
(b)  the date on which you want your maternity leave to begin;
(c)  the week in which your baby is expected to be born.
The notification of maternity leave form, available from the personnel department, should be used for this purpose. When submitting this form you should enclose a Form MAT B1 signed by your doctor or midwife.

3.1.4  The personnel department must be informed of the date of childbirth.

3.1.5  If you return to work at the end of your basic maternity leave you do not need to give notice of the date of your return. If you want to return to work before the end of your basic maternity leave, you must give 7 days' advance notice in writing, specifying the date of your return. Failure to give the correct notice where required could result in your return to work being delayed until the 7 day notice period or your basic maternity leave has expired.

### 3.2   Extended maternity leave

If you have completed 2 years' service at the start of the eleventh week before the expected week of childbirth, you are entitled to take a further period of maternity leave and return to work at any time until the end of 29 weeks from the Sunday before your child is born. The terms and conditions are the same as for basic maternity leave with the following additions:-

3.2.1   At the same time as giving the notification required by paragraph 3.1.3 you must indicate in writing your intention to take extended maternity leave.

3.2.2   You must give 21 days' advance notice in writing of the date on which you want to return from extended maternity leave. The company reserves the right to postpone your return by up to 4 weeks, in which case you will be notified in writing of the reasons for the postponement and the date on which you should return.

# 4   Statutory maternity pay (SMP)

4.1   If you have at least 26 weeks' service by the end of the fifteenth week before the expected week of childbirth, you will be entitled to receive SMP whether or not you intend to return to work.

4.2   SMP is payable for a maximum of 18 weeks beginning with the first week of your maternity leave. It is divided into two rates as follows:

(a)   For the first 6 weeks of your maternity leave, SMP is paid at the rate of 90 per cent of your salary.

(b)   For the remaining period of up to 12 weeks, SMP is paid at the lower statutory rate which is currently £52.50. The rate payable at any particular time can be obtained from the personnel department.

4.3   To claim SMP you must give 21 days' notice in writing of your intention to be absent from work on maternity grounds. If you are unable to give 21 days' notice, you should give as much notice as possible. If you intend to take maternity leave, you need only provide the written notice referred to in paragraph 3.1.3 above, otherwise you should ask the personnel department for a form for this purpose.

4.4   If you do not qualify for SMP you may be entitled to state maternity allowance, and you should contact the Personnel Department for details.

# 5   Contractual benefits during maternity leave

5.1   During basic maternity leave, or during the first 14 weeks of extended maternity leave, you will be entitled to your usual contractual benefits (including accrual of holiday entitlement) with the exception of your normal salary.

5.2   Pension contributions, where applicable, will be continued during the periods referred to in paragraph 5.1 provided you maintain your contributions.

# A Co Ltd

## Notification of Maternity Leave Form

To:        The Personnel Department

From:

I confirm that:

1    I am pregnant

2    I want my maternity leave to begin on [                               ].

3    My child is expected to be born in the week starting Sunday [                    ].

I enclose a form MAT B1 signed by my doctor/midwife.

4    (i)    *I will be taking basic maternity leave only; or

      (ii)    *I am entitled to and wish to take extended maternity leave.

* delete as appropriate.

Signed . . . . . . . . . . . . . . . . . . . . . . . . . . . . . . .

Dated . . . . . . . . . . . . . . . . . . . . . . . . . . . . . . .

# Appendix 4

## Useful Addresses

Central Office of the Industrial
Tribunals (England and Wales)
Southgate Street
Bury St Edmunds
Suffolk IP33 2AQ
Tel: 01284 762 300
Fax: 01284 706 064

The Commission for Racial Equality
(CRE)
Elliott House
10/12 Allington Street
London SW1E 5EH
Tel: 0171 828 7022
Fax: 0171 630 7605

The Equal Opportunities Commission
(EOC)
Overseas House
Quay Street
Manchester M3 3HN
Tel: 0161 833 9244
Fax: 0161 835 1657

EOC Wales
Caerwys House
Windsor Lane
Cardiff CF1 1LB
Tel: 01222 343 552
Fax: 01222 641 079

EOC Scotland
Stock Exchange House
Nelson Mandella Place
Glasgow G2 1QW
Tel: 0141 485 833
Fax: 0141 248 5834

For more information on the
Disability Discrimination Act (DDA)
contact:
The Department for Education and
Employment
DP2 Level One
Caxton House
Tothill Street
London SW1H 9NF
Tel: 0345 622633
Fax: 0345 622611

National Disability Council (NDC)
6th Floor
The Adelphi
1–11 John Adam Street
London WC2N 6HT
Tel: 0171 712 2099
Fax: 0171 712 2075

HMSO Publications Centre (mail, fax
and telephone orders only)
PO Box 276
London SW8 5DT
Tel: 0171 873 9090
     0171 873 0011 (general enquiries)
Fax: 0171 873 8200

For local Planning, Assessment and
Counselling Teams under the
Employment Service, see local
telephone directory

Employers' Forum on Disability
60 Gainsford Street
London SE1 2NY
Tel: 0171 403 3020
Fax: 0171 403 0404

Northern Ireland Disability Council
(NIDC)
Department of Health and Social
Services
Social Policy Branch
Room 3A Dundonald House
Upper Newtownards Road
Belfast BT4 3SF
Tel: 01232 524 997
Fax: 01232 524 733

Employers' Forum on Age
Astral House
1268 London Road
London SW16 4ER
Tel: 0181 679 1075
Fax: 0181 679 6069

# INDEX

direct, 25–26
employees, 32, 35
employers, 30
  vicarious liability of, 31
employers' associations, 33
employment agencies, 34–35
employment outside UK, 43
exemptions, 38–44
forms of, 25
genuine occupational qualification,
  38–44
harassment See Harassment
indirect, 26–28, 69–70
job applicants, 35
legislation, 23–24
liability for acts of, 30–35
marital, 28–29
married couples, 43
men, against, 25
mobility See Mobility
partnerships, liability of, 32
pensions See Pensions
personal welfare and educational
  services, provision of, 42–43
physiology, 39
police, 37
pressure to commit an act of
  discrimination, 247–248
  privacy or decency, 40–41
qualifying bodies, 33–34
self-employed, 36
sexual orientation See Sexual
  orientation
single sex establishment, 42
sport, 43

trade unions, 33
transsexuals See Transsexuals
victimisation See Victimisation
vocational training bodies, 34
Sexual orientation, 261–263,
  unfair dismissal, 265–266
Short lists
  *See* Recruitment

Terms and conditions of employment,
  contents of, 115–117
  hours of work *See* Hours of work
  mobility *See* Mobility
  transfer of undertakings *See* Transfer
    of undertakings
Training,
  customised, 107–108
  disabled people, 159
  positive action, 108
  pre-employment, 107
  pre-recruitment, 107
Transsexuals, 263–266
Transfer of undertakings, 277–280
Transfers,
  duties, to other, 160

Victimisation,
  avoiding claims of, 179–180
  definition, 179
  disabled people, 56–57, 180
  private households, 180
  racial, 8
  sexual, 29–30
  See also Harassment

.